FUTURISTS
and
COMMITMENTS

DUSTY HUGHES

faber and faber

LONDON · BOSTON

First published in 1986 by
Faber and Faber Limited
3 Queen Square London WC1N 3AU

Phototypeset by Wilmaset Birkenhead Wirral
Printed in Great Britain by
Redwood Burn Ltd Trowbridge Wiltshire
All rights reserved

British Library Cataloguing in Publication Data

Hughes, Dusty
Futurists and Commitments
I. Title
822'.914   PR6058.U34/

ISBN 0–571–13778–4

To the memory of my father,
Harold Hughes (d. 21 February 1986) –
a brilliant teacher

CONTENTS

Introduction to *Futurists* and *Commitments*   *page* 9

Futurists   13

Commitments   89

INTRODUCTION TO *FUTURISTS*
AND *COMMITMENTS*

After a grisly two-year apprenticeship directing in Birmingham, I came back to London in 1972 and repossessed my flat in Fulham. At the time there were regular weekly meetings in a well-known television director's house organized by a prominent left wing party (scrupulously painted by Trevor Griffiths in 'The Party') 'to try and get a dialogue going on the left'. The meetings were much more successful at tapping the enormous imaginative energy of the actors, film makers, writers and painters who came to them to defend their bourgeois ideas against the fierce materialism of the hard left. The party both despised us and desired us. The atmosphere was a little creepy. Still, the movement had enormous energy and put on a Pageant of Working Class History for an audience of 10,000 at the Wembley Empire Pool. It was a strange and exhilarating experience working on this gigantic play with a mixed cast of professional actors and working class families from Jarrow, Merthyr Tydfil and Manchester. You could hear well-known actresses being ticked off for swearing in front of the wives of Welsh miners. But after three hours of the performance, when the distant homuncule figure of Karl Marx stood up in spotlight to introduce himself and begin the section of the play known as 'Marx, Engels and the British Labour Movement', the entire audience, including hostile reporters from the *News of the World* looking for secret arms caches, stood and cheered for what seemed an epoch.

The couple who introduced me to these glamorous and contentious events were already members of the organization and they soon, fatefully, became my lodgers. I had no guilt about my lack of interest in politics. But politics, in the shape of two personable and talented people, had moved in with me, and I was politicized in the kitchen.

This was the time of Saltley Gates, the Miners' Strike, the Power Workers Work to Rule and the Three Day Week. The party newspaper, already piling up in pyramids in the hall, talked of the coming collapse of the West's entire economic system. And in truth things didn't look good at all. To someone without even the vaguest grounding in economic theory, they seemed apocalyptic. The impression of imminent disintegration lasted for a few months. I read everything I could about the 1917 Revolution. Images from the Russian Revolution and that year of activism are now bonded together in my consciousness. I finished Volume One of *Das Kapital*. I sold the paper outside Fulham Power Station. During the rail strike, I drove all night in my battered mini to deliver the paper round the North of England. I disagreed with my comrades about almost everything. At the time, nobody seemed to mind. But I think I must have known I was never going to make the transformation from a fellow traveller into a good Bolshevik.

People sitting around talking about the revolution seemed comical and bootless. Actually doing something about it, magically, re-created the world. It was a good lesson to learn. Change became a tangible thing. It was easy to think that there was a remorseless logic between the hard work of the organization and the chaos which poor Edward Heath was doing his best to control. Was London becoming Petrograd? The cold was certainly colder, the needs more desperate, the divisions sharper. The Thames began to look like the Neva. After a year of fruitless disagreement I finally had a party card pushed into my hand. Lying in bed with chicken pox and a temperature of 104° I was in no condition to argue. 'We're recruiting all sorts of tendencies now. We're becoming a mass revolutionary party. We're nothing like as fussy as we used to be.' It should have been the beginning, in fact it was the end.

I had stayed still for a moment too long and grey objectivity had returned. And so alas had Harold Wilson. The death of my girlfriend's father gave me an excuse to escape to Putney. I left the Jesuits of the Left in charge of the flat. A few years later, when *Commitments* opened in London, the reviewer for the party paper sneaked into a preview. It had been re-named and devoted a lot of space to horse racing tips. On the press night a party member sold more papers outside the theatre than I had in my entire time as a revolutionary. When the curtain went up half the audience had already read the review. It had been awarded a double page centre spread, with a headline that blared out: HUGHES'S POLITICS OF DESPAIR!

I discovered Gorky and Mayakovsky in those days of possibilities. I saw the shadowy equivalents of their struggles acted out in that peculiar climate of politics and showbusiness.

The starting point for *Futurists* was the poet Nikolai Gumilyov. He was a very fine poet and the first writer to be shot in the Soviet Union after the Revolution; a few years before Stalin began to do it for sport. There were stories about Gorky's involvement which either cast him in the role of a tortured father-figure, or as the tragically compromised literary commissar he became in the thirties. Had he cried and coughed up blood when he heard the news of Gumilyov's death? Or had he repeatedly refused to intervene with Lenin? And if so, what had happened to the friendship with Lenin which had survived so many years of differences and upheaval? In trying to answer the question I discovered a world of tribal artistic movements fighting in bizarrely named night clubs. There were characters left over from the past, preserved in aspic (like Anna Akhmatova). And there was Gorky, the greatest living Soviet writer, now a sort of one- man arts council with the power of life and death over the starving and largely despised intellectuals. It seemed a society in which, despite the new imperative of history, difficult moral questions were being posed over and over again. (How different from Earl's Court, vintage 1973.) It was a society in which change was happening at such vertiginous speed that the writers, the most sensitive instruments, were thrown off-balance. Some, like Mandelstam, regained their equilibrium and fought through to an inevitably tragic, but heroic end. And others, like Mayakovsky, who should have been for ever in the vanguard, were swept away by mediocrity. Above all it seemed to me to be the opposite, a mirror image, of the world of *Commitments* where the struggles though no less alive than in 1921, were only laughed at by history.

Futurists is finally about the indestructibility of poetry. It is a musical which has poems for songs, and in which poetry is the main character. The translations of the poems are my own free versions, except of course where the characters (Briuchkov, Yagodin) are purely fictional.

DUSTY HUGHES

FUTURISTS

THE CHARACTERS

AVERBACH (Leo)
YAGODIN
MAXIM GORKY (Alex)
MARINA
GUMILYOV (Kolia)
ELENA
BRIUCHKOV
AKHMATOVA (Anna)
LILI BRIK
KUFTIK (Victor)
TUMIN
MAYAKOVSKY (Volodya)
MANDELSTAM (Osip)
NADEZHDA (Nadia)
BLOK (Alexander)
PETROV
ROMANOV
STAVSKY
FIRST SAILOR (Lev)
SECOND SAILOR (Georgi)
TROFIMOV (in *The Cherry Orchard*)
ANYA (in *The Cherry Orchard*)
LENIN (Ilyich)/Gardin
BOOMSTRA
PEOPLE at The Stray Dog
GUESTS at Gorky's
PROLETCULTISTS
ACCORDIONIST

Futurists was first performed at the Cottesloe Theatre, London, on 17 March 1986. The cast was as follows:

AVERBACH	Fred Pearson
YAGODIN	Mark Jax
MAXIM GORKY	David Calder
MARINA	Caroline Bliss
GUMILYOV	Jack Shepherd
ELENA	Miranda Foster
BRIUCHKOV	Ian Bartholomew
AKHMATOVA	Charlotte Cornwell
LILI BRIK	Clare Higgins
KUFTIK	Jasper Jacob
TUMIN	Julian Fellowes
MAYAKOVSKY	Daniel Day Lewis
MANDELSTAM	Roger Lloyd Pack
NADEZHDA	Harriet Thorpe
BLOK	Christopher Guinee
PETROV	Colin Stinton
STAVSKY	John Priestley
ROMANOV	Peter Blythe
FIRST SAILOR	Peter Dineen
SECOND SAILOR	Michael Crompton
TROFIMOV	Michael Crompton
ANYA	Miranda Foster
LENIN	Peter Blythe
BOOMSTRA	John Priestley

Director	Richard Eyre
Designer	William Dudley
Lighting	Peter Radmore
Music	Dominic Muldowney

ACT I

The set is bare except for gauze and leaves and dappled light; the atmosphere autumnal. The light grows into a spotlight on the face of a young bearded man, scruffily dressed. He speaks intensely, polemically.

TROFIMOV: There *is* a future in which we'll find solutions to the problems that confront us. But we'll only achieve it by relentless struggle. Here, now, in Russia there are so few who are engaged in that conflict. The greater part of the intelligentsia seek nothing, do nothing and appear congenitally incapable of work of any kind . . .
    (The light comes slowly up. The MAN *is in fact talking to a woman. It is* The Cherry Orchard *at the end of Act II;* TROFIMOV *and* ANYA.*)*

ANYA: Why do I care less about the cherry orchard than I used to? There was nothing dearer in the world than our cherry orchard.

TROFIMOV: Our orchard is the whole of Russia. This vast amazing continent. Think of all the wonderful places in it. And remember that your father owned serfs. He owned other human lives, human souls, Anya. If you look carefully you can still see them hanging from the branches of your cherry orchard and their dead voices whispering in the leaves. You've always lived off the backs of others, all your ancestors have and that's what . . . that's what . . .
    (He stops and turns upstage, frozen.)
    (Stage whisper) What's the matter?

ANYA: *(Trying to cover up)* Our house hasn't really been ours for a very long time.
    (Pig sounds from behind the gauze.)
    (Prompting) That's what has finally destroyed them . . .
    (Suddenly the stage is invaded by a cheering, shouting horde of people dressed in rags or workers' clothes, or just outrageously. The Chekhov set is torn down and banners which shout out and challenge the audience are flown in. The Moscow Art Theatre

actors flee. At the head of the group, advancing threateningly, MAYAKOVSKY, *a large dominating man with a booming voice, pointing dramatically beyond the footlights.* TUMIN *the proprietor, slips into the spotlight to introduce each poet. An ex-character actor in his late forties, in evening dress and a buttonhole. His hair is shiny and his manner is ingratiating.*)

TUMIN: Mayakovsky.

MAYAKOVSKY: This is to you!
Gloomy gluttonous actors
Squealing down the years
Shaking the dumps called theatres
With 'Romeo, Romeo!'
And buckets of briny tears.

This is to you!
Chalky, porcine painters
Gorging and giggling with a passion
Secreted in your studios
Hoarding bosoms and blossoms
Like they're going out of fashion!

This is to you!
Fig-leaf fond and mystical
Furrowed foreheads sublime
Futuristical
Imagistical
Acmeistical
Gummed up in the cobwebs of rhyme!

This is to you!
Proletcultists
Patching Pushkin's togs.
Swapping your smooth hair cuts
For hay stacks
Patent leather for peasant clogs!

This is to you!
Prancing, or pooping on the pipes
Abandoned creatures
Pretending you're on our side
Privately on the other
Yearning for a hot hand-out
From your earth mother.

I am warning you.
Cut out the trifles
And the crap
Before you get a slap
From the end of a rifle!
(*Blackout. Banners go. The walls of the theatre become a gigantic mural of conflicting styles: the chaotic riches of Russian art at the beginning of the century. The auditorium has become the Stray Dog Café. It is a basement and people enter from above down a huge spiral staircase. To one side of the stage throughout is a gigantic stove. There is a grand piano decorated with fantastic Futurist designs.* KUFTIK, MAYAKOVSKY, LILI BRIK *and* AVERBACH *come on.* AVERBACH *is pale and intense.* LILI *is a beautiful fashionably-dressed, futurist* femme fatale. KUFTIK *is in evening dress, is wearing make-up and has mathematical symbols on both cheeks. He sits down at the piano.* AVERBACH *looks at him half-amused.*)

KUFTIK: (*In spotlight, at piano*)
This is the 'Stray Dog' Café
Poets and painters at play.
The Revolution
Is almost won.
In Petrograd
It's fun, it's fun, it's fun!

MAYAKOVSKY: (*In spot*) To you!
Prancing, or pooping on the pipes
Abandoned creatures
Pretending you're on our side
Privately on the other
Yearning for a hot hand-out
From your earth mother.

I am warning you.
Cut out the trifles
And the crap
Before you get a slap
From the end of a rifle!

TUMIN: Akhmatova.
AKHMATOVA: (*In spot*)
    It will sear you at the start
    As if to cold winds you were bare
    Then drop down into your heart
    Just a heavy, salty tear
MAYAKOVSKY: (*In spot*) Cut it out.
    Forget it.
    Spit
    On rhymes
    Roses
    Arias
    Hearts
    And every other sort of shit
    Out of the arsenals of the arts.
    No one cares about
    Your bleeding hearts!
TUMIN: Mandelstam.
MANDELSTAM: (*In spot, carrying an umbrella*)
    To read only children's books
    To dream only childlike dreams
    Have grown-up burdens melt, and free
    This deep devouring sorrow.

    I am mortally sick of existence.
    Life gives me nothing to sow
    But I love my poor bare earth
    It's the only land I know.

    In gardens out of time I played
    On a simple wooden swing
    And through a distant feverish haze
    The tall dark firs closed in.

MAYAKOVSKY: (*In spot*) Can you hear it?
Steam engines groaning
The wind whistling
Through the cracks in the floor
'Bring us coal from the Don!
Metal workers!
Mechanics!'
And wounded steamers
On every river
Howl out
'Bring us oil from Baku!
Bring us new forms!' they call.
And we sit around arguing
About the meaning of it all!

You're not fools
Yet you mass round 'maestros'
Mouths agape
Waiting for pearls
Like cows chewing cud.
Comrades!
Wake up!
Give us new art
To drag the republic out of the mud!

(*Enormous response from the club. Applause, cheers. He pauses, acknowledges the audience as* BLOK *appears*.)
Comrades, I defer to this man: Alexander Blok.
(BLOK *comes up, diffidently, from the back. He is in his late forties, stooped, and wearing a suit. He gets to the stage, seems short of breath.* BLOK *shuffles his papers unhurriedly. Looks over his pince-nez at* MAYAKOVSKY.)

BLOK: I'm sorry, Volodya that you're rhyming trifles with rifles. I'm sorry for both of us that we have to settle for trifles.

MAYAKOVSKY: Will you read 'The Twelve' for us?
(MAYAKOVSKY *smiles shyly, goes.* CLUB MEMBERS *shout 'Read "The Twelve"!'*)

BLOK: I'm sorry . . . I can't read 'The Twelve' for you . . . I've never been able to read it in public . . . and now I don't

have the breath for it. Something else. (*Fiddles in pocket.*) I
was described in a journal the other day as an old man . . .
I'm forty-one. But anybody born more than ten years ago is
old these days.

(*He finds the paper. A pause.* BLOK *reads, controlling his
breath with effort, making a calm low sound.*)

Those who were born in stagnant years
Remember the past so dimly.
We the children of Russia's awesome years
Have lost the power to forget.

The years are reduced to ashes.
Is it a beacon's light? Or madness gleaming
From days of war and days of freedom
That on our pallid faces casts a crimson shadow?

We are mute. The tocsin bells
Have sealed lips, smothered voices
And in our once exalted souls
There is only a lethal emptiness.

(BLOK *folds his notes absently and gets down. He looks sad and
troubled. He crosses the stage and exits straight away.*
AVERBACH *jumps up on to the stage.*)

AVERBACH: Comrades, there are urgent theoretical problems
which must be thrashed out. I have taken this liberty of
preparing an agenda which we hope you will find
acceptable.

(*The* PROLETCULTISTS *start handing out leaflets.*)

TUMIN: No!

(TUMIN *intercepts them and tries to take the leaflets away.*)

LILI: Are you speaking as an individual?

AVERBACH: I never speak as an individual. I am mandated to
say what I have to say. By the whole Proletcult movement.

LILI: Go ahead.

AVERBACH: We want you to join us. Unequivocally and publicly.

(*A silence.*)

LILI: That's not possible. We don't feel there is any common
ground between us.

22

AVERBACH: The enemy is looking for every sign of weakness or faintheartedness. He wants to put the clock back at the first opportunity. If we were to fight together he wouldn't have a chance.

LILI: Perhaps you're right. We should fight together.

AVERBACH: I'm pleased you think so, comrade. I've often thought that we were too factional. Too concerned with our own public profiles.

LILI: We are still fighting pre-revolutionary skirmishes . . . (AVERBACH *nods vigorously*.) . . . with pre-revolutionary weapons.

AVERBACH: Yes, yes, this is our argument precisely.

LILI: So you can join *us*.
(AVERBACH *is ambushed*. MAYAKOVSKY, *who has been brooding silently, chuckles*.)

MAYAKOVSKY: I worry about you, Leo. I think you're spending too much time in meetings.

AVERBACH: I don't see why this should worry you, Volodya.

MAYAKOVSKY: It's having a devastating effect on your complexion. You should get out more.

AVERBACH: There are a lot of things we have to sort out.

MAYAKOVSKY: You mean you want to subject the Futurist movement to a lot of meetings like this?

AVERBACH: The proletarian writers would like you to put your considerable weight behind them.

MAYAKOVSKY: I'm too busy putting my considerable weight behind the proletariat.

AVERBACH: I don't see the distinction.

MAYAKOVSKY: You're not – how shall I put it – a member of the proletariat yourself. Collecting folk ballads in obscure parts of the Urals doesn't qualify you. Though I did hear that in nineteen nine you once actually sat down to a meal with a peasant.

AVERBACH: I think you'll see later that you're being foolish and vindictive.

MAYAKOVSKY: I'm a poet, not a politician.

LILI: Volodya, we must stay and talk this out.

23

MAYAKOVSKY: No.

(MAYAKOVSKY *leaves, taking most of the* FUTURISTS *with him.*)

AVERBACH: The proletariat are there to join. We put ourselves at their disposal. It's only possible to do this if one drops certain individualistic concepts. I will leave you for the time being. I'm glad I've had a chance to see where you all spend your time. (*Looks about.*) I didn't realize that salons still existed. It's amazing how resilient literary society is. We'll let things take their course. The Proletcult movement is growing very quickly. I think we may find we have things in common. The joke you played at the Moscow Art Theatre was much appreciated. People like Stanislavsky carry on as if the Revolution had never happened. I'm told there are more furs and jewels in the audience than there were in 1913. (*Looks at* KUFTIK.) But this place on the other hand should be preserved, at least for the time being. It's a curiosity. Comrades . . .

(*He nods, goes. The club empties.* BRIUCHKOV, *a pale ragged young man, crosses the stage.* TUMIN *is doing accounts at a table.* LILI *and* KUFTIK *still there.*)

BRIUCHKOV: Excuse me, you said I could read when the club was empty.

TUMIN: Let's hear you then.

BRIUCHKOV: I am the colour of the New Age
No longer brittle
Like the dried pips
Of an orange
Setting in splendour
In the nocturne sky
But the stately blue tips
Of a steel-grey pylon.

TUMIN: (*Bored*) Splendid.

BRIUCHKOV: The ending is rather more . . . (*He gestures, wanly.*)
And I will whistle
Like a

24

Boiling kettle
To drive engines
With my breath!

TUMIN: Splendid. (*Turns to* LILI, *anxiously*.) Lili, dear . . .
Where's Mayakovsky?

LILI: How should I know?

TUMIN: I thought you were lovers.

LILI: How could you suggest such a thing? I'm a married
woman.
(*She crosses to him, holds out her hand. He bends to kiss it. She
slaps his face. Goes.* KUFTIK *trills on the piano.* BRIUCHKOV
goes after TUMIN.)

BRIUCHKOV: What do you think?

TUMIN: If the public will listen to you, you're good.

BRIUCHKOV: If there's anything I can do here, any odd jobs. I'll
clean out the lavatories. I can do anything.

TUMIN: Don't you have another job?

BRIUCHKOV: I help a bit at 'World Literature'. (*Proud of this.*)
For Maxim Gorky. But . . . well it's just for soup. I met
him . . . last week. He put a hand on my shoulder . . . He's
a great man.

TUMIN: Are you a good Futurist? (BRIUCHKOV *looks blank.*)
You know who the Futurists are don't you?
(KUFTIK *balances a chair on his teeth and walks around the
club.*)

BRIUCHKOV: I don't know. I come from Voronezh, you see. Do
you know it?

TUMIN: Er . . . yes. I do. (*He smiles at* BRIUCHKOV *benignly.*)
This is a Futurist club. We like the Futurists because
they're talented and because they have style like Victor over
there. One day the Bolsheviks are going to say that
Futurism is the movement closest to the revolutionary spirit
and sweep the others aside.

KUFTIK : They don't show any signs of it.

TUMIN: They're much too busy to bother at the moment. The
Proletcultists are our particular enemy. They're the ones
who walk around with balalaikas and call themselves
narodniks but now they tend to go around with caps on and

look like workers which they aren't. They think all art
should be simple so that workers can understand it. We get
real workers here too, confusing, but you can usually tell
them from the Proletcult unless they're actually members of
the Proletcult which is unlikely. The Proletcult hate us
because the workers actually prefer Futurism even if they
don't understand it yet, and they decorated all the best
trains during the civil war. Vous comprenez?

BRIUCHKOV: I think so . . .

TUMIN: Anybody who looks more or less normal is probably a
Symbolist, though they're mostly dead or nearly dead like
poor Alexander Blok whose performance we've slept
through this evening. Or they might be the Acmeists, who
were the chic thing in the salons of Petersburg before the
war. Then there are the Everythingists and the Nothingists.
You can't tell them apart usually. And so on, and so on.
You'll get the hang of it. I can't give you any money, but
there's plenty to do. And there are always people here
who'll show you where to scrounge a crust. All right young
feller?

(MANDELSTAM *and* NADEZHDA *enter from above.*

MANDELSTAM *is tall and has the bearing of a supertramp or
the king of the gypsies with ostentatiously patched trousers
contrasting strangely with a rolled umbrella.* NADEZHDA *is
wearing a Bohemian striped pyjama suit covered with splashes
of oil paint.*)

TUMIN: We're closed! (*Sees who it is.*) Osip, Nadezhda; there's a
gleam in your eye.

MANDELSTAM: I am a Jew. I come from a line of horsebreeders
and nomads and I shall curse you through seven generations.

TUMIN: Why on earth would you want to do that? (*Goes to*
NADEZHDA.) Little Nadia! (*She allows the embrace, coolly.*)
Quite right, you mustn't trust me. I'm just as bad as ever.

MANDELSTAM: (*To* TUMIN) Somebody is putting it about that
I've stopped writing. Somebody is spreading a rumour that
I've gone silent.

TUMIN: Why should anyone want to do that? You haven't, have
you?

26

MANDELSTAM: Never. Never.

NADEZHDA: Gumilyov was here last week. He said everybody was talking about it.

TUMIN: What an extraordinary thing. Of course, there's always gossip. You know what poets are like when they get together.

MANDELSTAM: It's as if all the poetry I'd ever written and had published and all the articles . . . none of them had ever existed. It's as if *I* had never existed. Whenever a publisher deigns to meet me he says 'Good lord, Osip, I thought you were dead' or, 'I'd heard the Revolution had made you too depressed to write'. but I do exist, Kostya. Look! Here! I haven't emigrated. And I'm not depressed. I'm angry.

TUMIN: (*Nervously*) Yes I can see that. There you are. But my dear friend you know how obsessed we all are about emigration. 'Have you heard so and so has gone to Paris' . . . 'Oh, it's only a holiday!' . . . 'What? A ten-month holiday!'

MANDELSTAM: Who is the rat? Who started these rumours? Mayakovsky?

TUMIN: Not Volodya, never . . . he would never start rumours.

MANDELSTAM: Perhaps it was Gorky. People always repeat what Gorky said.

TUMIN: Alexei Maximovitch is above that kind of thing.

MANDELSTAM: Are you sure? I seem to be the only writer in Russia who doesn't have a ration by the good grace of the great man.

TUMIN: Think how many lives that man has saved. We are all of us deeply, deeply in his debt. I for one won't listen to such slanders.

MANDELSTAM: Oh, he's a saint. A veritable saint. But he doesn't like me and I have no idea why. Politics? I welcomed the Revolution. I spent time in white jails in Kiev. We all hated the Romanovs. But do I have to pretend everything's perfect? Look at this city, it's a necropolis. No cars, no cabs, remember what it used to be like? Everyone shuffles about cramped up with malnutrition. Last night we stepped over a whole family of peasants in an alleyway off

Morskaya, all huddled together. All dead. From what? God knows. We hurried off pretty quickly.

TUMIN: Why would they want to say you were silent?

MANDELSTAM: Isn't silence anti-soviet? You know the species of bird that sits in the trees when the snows come and silently shivers? While the others do their best to make up the noise and warble optimistically.

TUMIN: People always get things wrong. What can I do?

MANDELSTAM: Tell everyone it's a slander. I am a poet. Somebody is trying to tread on my shadow. And not only me, but all of the Acmeists; Akhmatova and Gumilyov too.

TUMIN: I had hoped the age would reform you.

MANDELSTAM: What are we supposed to do to get published? You know everyone. Tell me! I can't earn a living any other way.

TUMIN: Keep your head down. You make too many enemies. And stop writing about the past. Nobody wants to hear about that any more. And stop being so pessimistic!

MANDELSTAM: What *incredible* rubbish you talk. Poetry is a plough. It turns time upside down. The past and the present and the future are always there whatever I write. And everything is not for the best and it is not now, nor will it ever be, the best of all possible worlds.

(MAYAKOVSKY *comes in from above. His cap is pulled down over his eyes and he's covering his face with a newspaper. He makes for the corner where* TUMIN *and the* MANDELSTAMS *are.* MAYAKOVSKY *makes to shake* MANDELSTAM's *hand but holds out two fingers, like a gun.*)

MAYAKOVSKY: Osip! What a surprise to find you here.

(MANDELSTAM *goes through with the handshake unconcernedly.*)

MANDELSTAM: Why a surprise, Volodya? I'm certainly not surprised to see you here.

MAYAKOVSKY: Oh, I'd heard we'd disappointed you. Thought you'd run off to Montmartre.

MANDELSTAM: You slanderous, decadent, anarchist thug. You have so little talent you have to borrow it.

TUMIN: (*To* MANDELSTAM) Come into my office. I'll find you something to eat. I don't want you to die on us.

(The club fills again. The FUTURISTS *and the*
PROLETCULTISTS *on opposite sides.* TUMIN *and the*
MANDELSTAMS *go off.* AVERBACH *now sits at the back
holding court at a table with some other* PROLETCULTISTS,
including YAGODIN *who has a balalaika and is singing a folk
song with which the others join in.* MAYAKOVSKY *in spotlight
again. Hushes the noise, but during the poem the*
PROLETCULTISTS *ignore him, talking quietly.)*

MAYAKOVSKY: Quiet – my kittens.
Up high
In the sky
Floated clouds
Four clouds
Hardly cloud crowds –
And one to three
Looked like men
Number four
Was a camel
And they all
Came adrift
And were joined
By a fifth
From which
Sprouted elephant
After elephant.
Were they met
By a sixth?
Who knows?
Pair by pair
Melted away
Into air.
And after them
Lolloping
(breaks off) Chomping –
I'm accustomed to silence when I perform.

AVERBACH: We apologize, Volodya. No hard feelings.
*(*MAYAKOVSKY *strolls over to the* PROLETCULTISTS' *table.)*

MAYAKOVSKY: *(To* AVERBACH) Of course not, Leo. So you're

joining us after all. I think you've made the right
decision.

AVERBACH: No, Volodya. We've just come in the hope of
hearing some poetry. Have you read the paper I left you?

MAYAKOVSKY: I'm a terrible reader, Leo.

AVERBACH: We want to thrash this one out. Sooner or later the
party is going to put its whole weight behind us. I wouldn't
want someone of your talent to be left out in the cold.

MAYAKOVSKY: Nice and warm in here, Leo!

YAGODIN: I've discussed your poems with our comrades and
they find them difficult. To understand.

MAYAKOVSKY: Then you should chose cleverer comrades.

AVERBACH: These are our proletarian comrades, Volodya. Do
you think the proletariat are stupid because they don't
understand your verse?

MAYAKOVSKY: No, they're just dumbfounded by being talked
down to by people like you.

YAGODIN: Some of them find the words you use distasteful.
They wouldn't like their womenfolk to hear about shit and
piss all the time.

MAYAKOVSKY: You don't know the working class as well as I
do. Where do you think I learnt my lavatorial humour? (*To*
YAGODIN) Come on Yagodin, let's hear what the Proletcult
are made of.

(*He pushes* YAGODIN *on to the stage.* YAGODIN *produces some
poems from a canvas bag and searches through them.*)

YAGODIN: 'The Death of Ivanov.'
Georgi Ivanov held the freezing bridge
Against the attacks of seventy white dogs.
Though wounded his head a bloody ridge
Through a white night of hellish fog
The worker Ivanov held the bridge.

And then it was Spring in Krasnokamsk
And the torrents swept down from the Pole
Marshing the pitted slopes to drown
Everything noble in that Ural hole.
(KUFTIK *comes to life at the piano and drowns* YAGODIN *out*

with crashing chords and discords before breaking into a jaunty tune. One of the PROLETCULT *crosses to pick a fight with him.*)

MAYAKOVSKY: Let the man be heard, Kuftik. Everyone has a right to be boring!

(KUFTIK *snatches the poem away.*)

KUFTIK: The death of 'The Death of Ivanov'!

(MAYAKOVSKY *becomes involved in the struggle as* KUFTIK *eats* YAGODIN's *poem. Suddenly, two loud bangs.* GUMILYOV *has entered dramatically, discharging two pistol shots into the air. Runs down the stairs and into the spotlight. He is an adventuror, a dandy with a shaven head and rings, but underneath he is a clever and serious man. The club appears to empty, most people are under the tables. Gradually they reappear.*)

GUMILYOV: Somebody once accused me of being an anarchist. Morons! I am not an anarchist. I am a monarchist! (*A gesture of mock horror.*) I am Gumilyov! Yes, you see, I can stand before you like the demon king and you can boo me. Do you know where this came from? (*Waves the gun.*) I bought it from a German in Somalia. You probably don't even know where Somalia is. It's in Africa. I went there to try and claim it for the Tsar. It always worried me that the Tsars weren't a bit more liberal. All this rather unnecessary mowing down of crowds in the street. I've always admired the British sort of monarchy. They don't have to do all that. They've got colonies so they can take it out on the natives instead of their own kind.

(*The people in the club have shrunk back again; are disappearing. The lights begin to narrow in on* GUMILYOV.)

Anyway it was a bit of a disaster in Somalia. I got a few good poems out of the experience. I dedicate this, with the right degree of irony, to the Russian Association of Proletarian Writers and all you great ego-Futurists . . .

We have forgotten that the word alone
Shone radiantly over the troubled world
And in the Gospel according to St John
The word of God unfurled.

31

We have made our frontier
The mere extremity of thought and action
And like dead bees in a deserted hive
Dead words smell of putrefaction.

(*During the poem a great cloth descends: a mural depicting the great fortress at Kronstadt, an ice-bound battleship and sailors.* GUMILYOV's *manner has changed. He is less aggressive, diffident almost. He is now lecturing directly to the audience.*)
I am a poet. As you may have gathered. Thanks to the good offices of the Commissariat of Education, I have invaded your ship to lecture to you on the subject of poetry. The last time I gave such a lecture I discovered that the sailors came almost exclusively from Georgia and understood not a word. (*Slight pause.*) You do, I see . . . I agreed to do this lecture for two important reasons. One. I am given a ration for doing it. Two. I was born here in the naval fort of Kronstadt. (*He pauses, produces his notes.*) A few years before the war against Germany, in which I fought and was wounded, I founded a movement called Acmeism. It is no coincidence that the three greatest living Russian poets are Acmeists: Osip Mandelstam, Anna Akhmatova and myself. (*A pause.*) But if we are to begin at the beginning of this century, which we now know was a kind of ending . . . we must begin with Blok. What can I tell you about Alexander Blok? He was part of a movement too, the Symbolist movement. He is five times greater now than Symbolism. Like most movements Symbolism was a paper fortress. What happened to it? Do you care? Well, I shall tell you anyway even if you don't understand a word. The Commissariat of Education shall get its kopeck's worth. Symbolism became swollen from the dropsy of great themes. It sealed up all words and images and put them to work in an endless liturgy. Take, for example, a rose and a sun, a dove and a girl. To the Symbolists none of these things are the least bit interesting in themselves. The rose is a likeness of a sun, the sun is a likeness of a rose, a dove – of a girl, and a girl – of a dove. An extremely awkward

situation arose. No one could move. Or stand up. Or sit down. One could no longer eat at a table because it was no longer simply a table. One could no longer light a lamp because it might signify unhappiness later. And so the movement died on its feet. With the birth of Acmeism, new blood began to course through the veins of Russian poetry. (*He stops, it is clearly hopeless.*) I think at this point, I'll leave the theory. Are there any questions? (*No response.*) Long live the Tsar! (*He bows quickly.*) Thank you gentlemen. (*He collects his papers, begins to go. Stops.*) Have you heard of Gorky? Good. That's something at least. . . . (*The lights change. The cloth flies out to reveal a table and a festive occasion.* GORKY's *apartment. Night.* GORKY *is at the head of a large gathering.* GUMILYOV *stands aside and addresses the party.* GORKY's *mistress and secretary* MARINA *is handing round vodka,* GUMILYOV *takes one. She is in her late twenties, glamorous and energetic.*)

GUMILYOV: Dear friends, we're all here to celebrate the birthday of a man who, more than anyone else, has demonstrated the virtues of a great human being . . . in impossible circumstances.

(GORKY *looks at the floor, wants him to stop.*)

Alex, we don't see eye to eye on a lot of things. For a start you don't like my poetry, or the poetry of any of my friends. Indeed it's very difficult for me to believe that you like poetry at all. (*Murmurs of disapproval.*) In matters of poetic taste you've always displayed the virtues of a novelist. (*Everyone silent, embarrassed.*) But for all that, there are many of us alive today who might not have been alive if Maxim Gorky had never existed. I salute you! May you live to be a hundred and never be bitten by a snake!

MARINA: A toast!

TUMIN: To a true humanitarian socialist!

AVERBACH: To Alexei Maximovitch!

MARINA: Alex, I have a surprise for you. Your birthday cake. (*An enormous cake is wheeled on.*)

GORKY: Now, Marina. This won't do at all. People are starving.

MARINA: It's made with nuts and carrots. There's absolutely nothing rationed in it.

(LILI BRIK *bursts out of the cake. She has a large sash which says '1921' on it. Everyone cheers.*)

GORKY: Lili you are magnificent! What a surprise! Am I that old? I'm not even half a century.

LILI: I was going to wear it at the New Year, but I never had the chance.

ALL: Speech! Speech!

GORKY: I suppose I ought to say something. Before the whole thing becomes too frivolous. When this terrible famine began, there was a danger that the whole culture, writers and scientists, people with very important specialized knowledge, might simply disappear. There was a danger that we might be completely cut off from the past . . . everything.

MAYAKOVSKY: I thought that was what the Revolution was trying to achieve.

GORKY: Of course, but we don't want to see brilliant poets digging latrine trenches. Or do you Volodya?

(MAYAKOVSKY *is suitably chastened.*) Because of this desperate situation I went to my old friend of twenty years, to Lenin, and as you know we've had our differences in the past, but this time he agreed with me. He gave me the resources and the rest is history. I'm exhausted. I haven't written a word for a year, but we have saved in human terms, for the future, riches that the grandest museum in the world couldn't hold. (*Applause.*) But of all the tasks I have, it is keeping writers alive that is the biggest nightmare. Some of you were barely alive before the Revolution. (*Laughter.*) – I want to make a toast too. I want you to raise your glasses to the man who I trust above all others, who has granted every request I've ever made to him however small and personal. To my old friend of twenty years, to Vladimir Ilyich Lenin!

(*All raise their glasses, affected by* GORKY'*s sincerity. The toast is murmured.* GORKY *begins to sing and eventually, everyone joins in. The song ends in a rousing chorus. Perhaps*

GUMILYOV *doesn't sing so enthusiastically but everyone is affected by the spirit of the years before the Revolution. There is a sense of community. The song is 'The Workers' Marseillaise'.*)
We renounce the ancient order
We shake its dust off our feet.
Golden idols are hateful to us
We despise the Tzarist court.
And the daylight of freedom will come.
Evil lies will perish for ever
And people will labour as one.
Our fight will never be contained
For we march together for the future.

So rise, you toiling folk!
'Gainst the foe you hungry men!

Ring out the call! The people's revenge!
Advance! Advance! Advance!
MAYAKOVSKY: Advance!
(*The real birthday cake arrives and is handed out.* BRIUCHKOV *comes in carrying a dozen copies of a new edition of* Faust.)
BRIUCHKOV: Excuse me for butting in like this but they told me you'd want to see these as soon as they came off. Ten copies of *Faust*.
GORKY: Good man! What's your name?
BRIUCHKOV: Briuchkov, comrade citizen.
(GORKY *snatches a book and shows it to the group.*)
GORKY: Look at this. The first from 'World Literature'. In a few years we're going to have every foreign classic in a first-class Russian edition. And keep all these bloody writers alive as well.
GUMILYOV: Until we all die from charity and an overdose of translation.
BRIUCHKOV: It's going to take a long time to get them all out. It's so cold that the ink keeps freezing on the paper and that makes the rollers jump.
GORKY: It's a wonderful effort.
BRIUCHKOV: We still have a problem getting paper . . .
GORKY: Oh to hell with that for today! Things always happen

eventually. It was much worse *before*. Let's get a copy off to Lenin. Make sure it goes priority. And when you've done that, come back and join us.

BRIUCHKOV: I'm not really dressed for this kind of thing.

(*All laugh.* GORKY *steps into the centre of the circle again.* BRIUCHKOV *goes.*)

GORKY: One more toast. (*Pause.*) By now all of you here, my closest friends, know that I've had a secret guest in my household for some weeks. I'd like to drink to a man . . .

ROMANOV: Oh no, Alex, please.

GORKY: . . . whose survival we hope will be a symbol of a new humanity in the Soviet Union. A liberal, humane man, who by an accident of birth was unlucky enough to be born a Grand Duke, but who has always supported revolutionary causes and who has had the courage to stay with us. To Gabriel Romanov!

ROMANOV: I am honoured. Thank you.

ALL: Speech!

(*All drink and say the toast.* ROMANOV, *a diffident man in his late forties, steps forward.*)

ROMANOV: I'm not going to make a speech but I'll tell you a story which may surprise you. My great-aunt was in Moscow when the Revolution broke out. She was eighty and she got it into her head that she wanted to go and visit her brother-in-law in Latvia. She always did at that time of year. So she sent her butler to the station to arrange for her private carriage as usual. But this time he came back rather quickly and said 'I'm sorry, ma'am, but they told me at the station that there weren't any private carriages any more and didn't I know there was a revolution going on.' My aunt was very upset about this. She was furious. So she sent the poor butler off to the Kremlin with a stinging note to Lenin. And Lenin received him. And he read the note and either he was amused by it or completely taken aback, because he gave the order for my aunt to have her carriage hitched up as usual. 'Well,' she said to the butler, 'I've got my carriage and I'm off!' And she stopped off here in Petrograd on the way, she had another house here, and discovered that her cousin had prudently hid her jewels under the floorboards, and she fished them out and sent them off to Lenin with a note saying she hoped it would help him win the war against the Germans.

(*Laughter and applause. The sound of accordion music off. All begin to go off.*)

MARINA: Let's all dance. Come on, Alex, I want you to have fun tonight.

GORKY: All right, all right. I'll come.

GUMILYOV: You've no power, Alex.

(*This holds* GORKY *back.*)

GUMILYOV: They're playing games with you.

GORKY: I have all the power I need. I have intervened for people on countless occasions. I have written to Lenin, telegraphed him, trudged off to the Kremlin to plead for some fool's life. He's never let me down.

GUMILYOV: Why should he? He wants to keep you happy. You have a lot of influence. You could use it better in opposition.

GORKY: Rebel against inhumanity. Rebel against injustice. But don't involve me in any more politics. My main concern is to make our writers the moral force.

GUMILYOV: You remind me of one of those monks of the Middle Ages whom the great princes used to keep for spiritual guidance. The princes felt purified by the relationship but carried on plundering as if there was no tomorrow. You're a kept monk, Alex.

GORKY: I remember you as a young man who considered it was the height of rebelliousness to claim he was a monarchist. The mask seems to have stuck, Kolia.

GUMILYOV: Will you give me sanctuary too, Alex? I may need it one day.

GORKY: You're not in any danger. You're a poet, Kolia. Nobody listens to a word you say.

GUMILYOV: It didn't keep Pushkin out of trouble.

GORKY: Perhaps the mistake would be to compare yourself with Pushkin. You Acmeists always thought too highly of yourselves.

GUMILYOV: You hate us. You always have done.

GORKY: No, Kolia. I don't hate you. I hate groups and circles that's all. Tiny gangs with outlandish manifestos who make a ridiculous hullaballoo. Look at these people who ruined the Chekhov play the other day. Mayakovsky's lot. Thought it was a good joke to cover a lot of pigs with axle grease and let them loose on the stage. Is that the future?

GUMILYOV: I worry about the future. Why do you think I invited Akhmatova and Mandelstam here tonight? I hope you don't mind. I wanted you to see how completely destitute they are. Neither of them has been published since the Revolution. You have a real hatred for spiritually inclined people, haven't you? Perhaps the grace of the saviour of our culture only falleth upon them of whom he approves.

(GORKY *is stunned for a moment, not sure how to respond to what he feels is a calumny*.)

GORKY: Akhmatova's husband has a ration and Mandelstam was given a job in the Commissariat of Education and left voluntarily. I welcomed them both into my home – they ate well. I hope you don't mean what you're implying, Kolia. If you mean it . . .

GUMILYOV: Akhmatova can hardly survive on her husband's ration when he spends most of his time away. In any case they're separating.

GORKY: I can't keep track of everyone. Particularly if they're too proud to come to me.

GUMILYOV: Show me a writer who isn't proud.

GORKY: Friend Mandelstam has given up writing completely by all accounts. He's apparently wandering around like a tramp crying out like Cassandra about the death of the old culture.

GUMILYOV: Who told you this?

GORKY: I was told, I was told.

(BRIUCHKOV *comes on. Hovers*.)

GORKY: My dear fellow Briuchkov. Join the dancing. You're a guest tonight.

BRIUCHKOV: Thank you, thank you. (*Goes*.)

GORKY: (*To* GUMILYOV) Two or three people told me.

GUMILYOV: I've seen that little mouse before.

GORKY: He's an informer. For the Cheka.

GUMILYOV: How do you know?

GORKY: Marina told me. (GUMILYOV *blank*.) My secretary.

GUMILYOV: How does she know?

GORKY: Because the Cheka sent her to spy on me. And they
    sent Briuchkov to spy on Marina.

GUMILYOV: Alex, be careful.

GORKY: It's only a game. They don't actually do anything.
    Remember what the old lot used to be like. You'd be lucky
    to keep your balls.

GUMILYOV: Get rid of her. How can you trust her?

GORKY: I saved her life. Her husband was shot in eighteen. She
    was too close to some English diplomats here. They got
    hold of her and she was very probably going to be shot
    during one of the panics. I made a fuss and they released
    her as long as I'd give her a job. After a week she blurted it
    all out. She has to report every week. But I can be sure of
    her. (*Pause.*) Pillow talk. (GUMILYOV *throws up his arms in
    despair and lets out a theatrical groan.*) Perhaps it's just the
    most delicious form of deceit. But I don't care. Look at me,
    Kolia, she's an aristocrat. She's rather beautiful, don't you
    think?

(MAYAKOVSKY *comes on.*)

MAYAKOVSKY: (*He looks out front.*) The sky's glowing over
    there. Did you hear the guns?

(MAYAKOVSKY *and* GORKY *look at each other.*)

They're going to smoke the sailors out of the fort before the
    ice melts.

GORKY: It's only a show of force. They'll negotiate a truce.
    Some of those men were on the *Aurora* when it bombarded
    the Winter Palace. Half of them are party members.

MAYAKOVSKY: Even the best people can turn against you.

GUMILYOV: They're demanding the right of peasants to sell
    their own produce. What can possibly be wrong with that?

MAYAKOVSKY: Because people are starving to death in the
    cities, so food has to be got out of their greedy little mits as
    fast as possible.

GORKY: But these sailors are heroes of the Revolution. The government will listen to them. The Bolsheviks will never fight their own. Or I've chosen the wrong side.

GUMILYOV: (*Quietly, listening*) That's artillery. They wouldn't be firing blanks would they, Alex?

(GORKY *turns and leaves, with a glance at the other two.* LILI *comes in.*)

MAYAKOVSKY: You're moving in with me tomorrow as we planned.

(GUMILYOV *bows, leaves.*)

LILI: I won't leave him. I can't.

MAYAKOVSKY: Don't be silly. We've decided.

LILI: You are my lover. You are the most important person in my life. But I won't let you devour me.

MAYAKOVSKY: You're moving in with me tomorrow. As we planned.

LILI: No. I'll keep a room, just one room in your apartment. And I'll visit you there from time to time.

MAYAKOVSKY: I need to be with you all the time. I can't split. I can't divide. I can't share. Not with Brik, not with anyone . . .

LILI: My husband tolerates the situation because he loves me and he loves you. It's our private business. But if it was suddenly all public it would humiliate him. And worse, it would break up the Futurists. People would take sides . . . our friends.

MAYAKOVSKY: But to fly in the face of the future is death. I am willing you to leave him and you will.

LILI: Will-power is not enough.

MAYAKOVSKY: If he loves me, he'll forgive me.

LILI: But other people will never forgive you. If you love me as much as you say you do, then we will always be together. There has to be something in this world that your talent and determination can't subjugate. We will carry on as we always did in our old Bohemian way. When I have to be with him, you can amuse yourself as you always do with one of your many admirers.

MAYAKOVSKY: And if I don't want to do that any more?

LILI: I don't belong to anyone. Don't you remember why we wanted the Revolution? Everyone should be free of all that bourgeois nonsense.

MAYAKOVSKY: That was a small part. The unimportant part.

LILI: It was important to me.

MAYAKOVSKY: It was shit.

LILI: If we can't escape the old dead rituals, if we can't lead, how will others ever learn? The Revolution will be stillborn if what happens between men and women doesn't change.

MAYAKOVSKY: You're the bourgeois, Lili Brik. (*She strikes out at him. He holds her wrists.*) It's over between us.

(AKHMATOVA *comes on with* GORKY; BRIUCHKOV *at a distance.* LILI *and* MAYAKOVSKY *go, separately.*)

AKHMATOVA: I'm glad to be able to pay my respects to you on your birthday.

GORKY: Gumilyov was suggesting you might not be the kind of person to come forward if you were suffering hardship of any kind.

AKHMATOVA: Oh, I've been able to survive quite well I think. Kolia was being over-concerned for my well being. Perhaps he feels guilty.

GORKY: Your . . . er, new husband still has his ration from the University?

AKHMATOVA: He does.

GORKY: I'm sure it would be possible to find you some work. Office work, I'm afraid.

AKHMATOVA: (*Laughs*) Thank you, no. People are very kind. And things can be sold. I've never believed in possessions. An empty apartment is perfect to work in and as my father often says to me, 'with your sins that's the best we can hope for'.

GORKY: Your father sounds very severe.

AKHMATOVA: You remind me of him sometimes. He called me a 'decadent poetess' once. And that was when I was still a girl and hadn't even begun to think about writing poetry.

GORKY: (*Slightly distant*) I'm glad there are no difficulties. Excuse me, I must go and join the rabble.

(GORKY *goes.*)

BRIUCHKOV: Excuse me . . .

AKHMATOVA: Yes?

(BRIUCHKOV *fiddles in his coat.* AKHMATOVA *waits patiently.*
BRIUCHKOV *produces a piece of paper. Clears his throat.*)

BRIUCHKOV: Anna Andreyevna Akhmatova, I salute you on
your birthday. You are the greatest Russian poet of our age.
Your poetry has sustained me through every hardship. I
fervently hope that with the Revolution, your poetry will
leap further out into the world, to the people and to
children. May you live to be a hundred.

(AKHMATOVA *inclines her head, smiles.*)

AKHMATOVA: Thank you, I'm overwhelmed.

BRIUCHKOV: (*Sitting*) I write a little verse myself. I'd hoped you
might find time to look at some of my stuff.

AKHMATOVA: After that how could I refuse?

BRIUCHKOV: This is something of a holy occasion for me. I'm
afraid I know everything about you.

AKHMATOVA: Do you? (*She looks at him intently.*) That's very
disconcerting.

BRIUCHKOV: I know everything you've written. Most of it by
heart. I feel I've known you for a very long time. I'm
negotiating with a small publishing house in Moscow.
They're hoping to bring out a slim volume, but you know
how long these things take.

AKHMATOVA: For ever.

BRIUCHKOV: I know your . . . er, N. S. Gumilyov. I believe
you and he were married once. I tried to get enrolled on his
poetry course, but I'm afraid I didn't make the grade.

AKHMATOVA: Poetry is so much a matter of taste, isn't it?

BRIUCHKOV: True. And of course there's always another time.
What is time, what is time . . .

(BRIUCHKOV *laughs nervously*)

I was told your last husband, the . . . er one after Gumilyov
. . . I was told he used to destroy your poems and then
claim it was a mistake.

AKHMATOVA: I always gave him the benefit of the doubt.

BRIUCHKOV: I noticed you and Gumilyov weren't exactly on
speaking terms.

AKHMATOVA: Did you? I'm merely being discreet. He's here with a girlfriend. She's rather young.

BRIUCHKOV: It must have been difficult for two poets to live together.

AKHMATOVA: It was difficult for us to live together. But not for that reason. Because we fought and were unfaithful to each other. He wanted me to be a ballet dancer. Now he rather respects my work.

BRIUCHKOV: And where is your son? You had a son together, didn't you?

AKHMATOVA: He's in Kiev, with my mother. I can't afford to feed him.

BRIUCHKOV: You lied to Gorky about getting a ration from your husband because you're too proud. It's a disgrace, Anna Andreyevna, that someone as eminent as yourself is reduced to selling your own carpets.

AKHMATOVA: What made you think it was my birthday? I was born in June.

BRIUCHKOV: (*Taken by surprise*) Oh . . . I checked it in the glossary at the House of Writers.

AKHMATOVA: It doesn't matter. (*Smiles sweetly.*) It can be my official birthday. Can I ask you a question?

BRIUCHKOV: I understand why you're a genius. Because you don't hide a thing. You bare your soul.

AKHMATOVA: Are you in love with me? (*Pause.*) Perhaps you're only in love with the me that you think is in my verse?

BRIUCHKOV: I'm sorry. I'm taking far too much of your time. I haven't really been invited.

AKHMATOVA: I'm sorry, I've embarrassed you. Don't go.

BRIUCHKOV: Thank you.

(*Bows stiffly.*)

There are some who might think that your poetry belongs to the past, to the old days and that we're finished with all that.

AKHMATOVA: (*Laughs*) I'm only thirty-five, you know. There's life in the old dog yet.

(*He goes.* GUMILYOV *comes on from the other side.*)

GUMILYOV: Be careful with admirers.

AKHMATOVA: Oh, he's harmless.

GUMILYOV: Did Gorky give you a ration?

AKHMATOVA: It was kind of you. But I don't want his charity.

GUMILYOV: I despair of you all. Mandelstam refuses to do anything but write. He's apparently applied to Gorky for a pullover and a pair of trousers. I don't even know if he's serious.

AKHMATOVA: Have you seen his trousers? (*A pause.*) Your son would like to see you and my mother would be happy if you want to go to Kiev and visit him.

GUMILYOV: In the spring I will of course.

AKHMATOVA: I don't see him enough either. (*Pause.*) Are you in trouble? You look hunted.

(*A pause.*)

GUMILYOV: I came to see you read the other evening on Kazánskaya. I'm sorry but I didn't stay behind.

AKHMATOVA: What did you think? Did I pass muster?

GUMILYOV: Yes. Muster passed. Seven poems at least without the pronoun 'I' and the verb to love.

(AKHMATOVA *throws her head back and laughs.*)

GUMILYOV: I used to hate all those faltering line endings. Like little handkerchiefs, poking out of the sleeve of your dress. You've changed.

(ELENA *comes on, sees* GUMILYOV.)

ELENA: Kolia!

(GUMILYOV *gestures her not to disturb them.*)

AKHMATOVA: Who is the girl?

GUMILYOV: One of my poetry students. Her father designs steam trains. I thought she'd be suitably functional for this kind of gathering.

(ELENA *in the shadows overhears this. The music stops.* MARINA *and* GABRIEL ROMANOV *also drift on.*)

I'm bored with her already.

ELENA: I hope I'm not interrupting anything.

AKHMATOVA: Hardly, if at all.

ELENA: Kolia!

(AKHMATOVA *wraps herself around* GUMILYOV. *They kiss.* ELENA *is frozen out.* AKHMATOVA *leaves. The music starts up again.*)

44

ROMANOV: You've exhausted me.

MARINA: Good.

(*There is a hammering at the door, off.*
GUMILYOV *looks at door. Takes out his gun. Another knock.*
Hands gun to ROMANOV.)

GUMILYOV: You will be a prisoner in your own country. Don't let them do that to you. Go to Finland quickly.

ROMANOV: I beg your pardon.

(*Knock.*)

VOICE: (*Off*) Cheka. Open up!

GUMILYOV: You can organize abroad. There are thousands waiting for a sign from you.

ROMANOV: Are you serious? (*Knock.*)

MARINA: I'll have to answer that.

GUMILYOV: Stand up for the motherland. Your blood is our blood.

ROMANOV: My dear friend, where the Romanovs are concerned blood is the one thing you shouldn't rely on. (ROMANOV *hands the gun back.*)
The reason I'm trying to get to Finland is because I've a disease which can be treated there. My wife and I are waiting for permission to leave. But don't misunderstand me, we have no intention of being used as a rallying point against the Bolsheviks. I've waited too long for nemesis to overhaul the family sleigh. You're drunk and I'm going to bed.

GUMILYOV: You are a half man. A homuncule.

ROMANOV: Oh very probably.

(ROMANOV *goes up the stairs. A* grand rond *fills the stage,*
danced (almost) ironically. GORKY *leads it and all the other*
characters join in. The stage swirls with rough energy and life.
As it finishes MARINA *comes on with two* CHEKA *officers,*
PETROV *and* STAVSKY.)

MARINA: Alex, I'm sorry . . .

PETROV: I have instructions to search this house for counter-revolutionaries.

(GORKY *goes over to the* CHEKA *officers.*)

GORKY: Comrades, I am Maxim Gorky.

PETROV: I know who you are. I have the strictest instructions.

GORKY: You have instructions to search my house? Who could possibly give you instructions to do that?

PETROV: I can't tell you that.

GORKY: You will have to show me somebody's signature on a piece of paper before you search my house.

PETROV: I'm afraid there wasn't time for that. This is much too serious.

GORKY: Obviously you don't have a warrant. In that case you can't search my house. I must remind you that I am a personal friend of Vladimir Ilyich Lenin so there are hardly likely to be any counter-revolutionaries here. As you can see, I'm holding a private birthday party with a few friends. (PETROV *and* STAVSKY *take in the party, the guests.*) Comrades, I insist you drink my health. Marina! (MARINA *gives them vodka.*)

STAVSKY: We only act on orders. If we gave everybody a fair hearing there'd be anarchy. People have been trying to say that these strikers are loyal workers, well maybe they are but do loyal workers listen to agitators and provocateurs? It's the same with these sailors. If they're the same glorious men of October then somebody's been getting at them. We've had a reputation for being a bit soft here in Petrograd if you get my meaning. There's still a few types, ex-army types, who want to do things by the book. But that's all going to change.

PETROV: I'd like to know the names of everyone here. It's just a little formality.

GORKY: Everyone in this house. . . ?

MAYAKOVSKY: Comrades. Do you know this mug shot? Or am I to accuse you of being a philistine?
(*He jumps up on the table.*)
The Revolution!
Is a Gillette razor!
Which slices through
Visionproud
Rock jealous
Two words

46

I up-mades.
Though personally
Cos of their raritee
I borrows my blades!

GUMILYOV: (*To* MAYAKOVSKY) That is an insult to poetry. A
crude parody. Take it back.
(*He gets up on the table opposite* MAYAKOVSKY. *Slaps his face
gently with a napkin.*)

MAYAKOVSKY: I challenge you.
(*He gets down, leaving* GUMILYOV *there. Pause.*
MAYAKOVSKY *exits.*)

GORKY: Don't be a fool, Kolia. Come on, my friends, I'll show
you round my apartment. There really isn't anything to
hide. Come on.
(GORKY *goes off with the two* CHEKA *men.* BRIUCHKOV *tags
on.* MARINA *looks concerned.*
Sound of window breaking. Two SAILORS *come on, with*
LILI. *One slightly wounded.* GUMILYOV *watches, getting
ready to leave.*)

SAILOR: Is this the house of Gorky? Maxim Gorky, the writer.

MARINA: Yes, it is.

SAILOR:⎫We were told it was safe.
LILI: ⎭They were trying to break in.

SAILOR: They're crushing the strike. The Red Army have gone
in against us sailors . . . against the fort, over the ice.

MARINA: What are you doing here?

SAILOR: We were on leave. We were in a bar. Take us in, Sir.
They're shooting at sailors . . . sailors anywhere. They said
Gorky was a good comrade. Will you help us?

LILI: We've got to treat that wound.

MARINA: What are you planning to do?

SAILOR: Hide somewhere until it all dies down and then get
back to our villages. I come from Saratov. They said it was
safe at comrade Gorky's.
(LILI *and* MARINA *look at each other.*)

LILI: Not at the moment.

MARINA: You'd better change those clothes. Come with me.
Quickly!

(*They go off, the music stops. Applause.* TUMIN *on.*
GUMILYOV *putting on his coat.*)

TUMIN: (*In blind panic*) I can't allow my club to be used as a doss house any more.

(GUMILYOV *looks up at* TUMIN *innocently.*)

You've got a perfectly good studio of your own. You can go back there.

GUMILYOV: I haven't paid the rent.

TUMIN: Don't be absurd, whoever heard of anyone paying rent these days? Anyway from now on you can't sleep in the 'Stray Dog'.

GUMILYOV: *You* do.

TUMIN: It's my club.

GUMILYOV: We've always been old friends, Kostya, haven't we?

TUMIN: You make me nervous, that's all. I never know what you're going to do next.

GUMILYOV: Believe me, I don't either.

TUMIN: (*Panic even worse.*) I've been trying to find a cab. It's absolutely impossible. Even with bribery.

GUMILYOV: Why don't you walk? Like everyone else.

TUMIN: You must be mad. There's a machine gun spraying the street.

GUMILYOV: You won't be any better off in a cab.

TUMIN: They move faster.

(TUMIN *goes.* ELENA *comes on. She looks nervous and distraught.*)

GUMILYOV: It's time for me to go. Alone, I'm afraid.

ELENA: Another tutorial? It's always struck me as odd, given your feelings about women and verse, that there should be so many women on your course.

GUMILYOV: Will you take a message to my deputy? At the Academy.

ELENA: Who are you going to see? Evgenia?

GUMILYOV: Tell him I've gone to Kiev. It's very urgent. Tell him and no one else. You do know where the Academy of Arts and Sciences is, don't you?

ELENA: You really think I'm dumb, don't you? I'll follow

48

you home and find out.

GUMILYOV: Believe me, home is one place I won't be going.
Will you do this for me, Elenotchka?

ELENA: And by the way I'm giving up poetry. I'm going to be a
film actress.

GUMILYOV: You're only blowing up bridges that you're too lazy
to cross. Would you do one other tiny thing? Let yourself
into my apartment. You've still got a key? Find my
warmest pair of trousers and give them to Mandelstam.

ELENA: Is this how you treated Akhmatova when you were
married?

GUMILYOV: Don't start that. Remember the message. And
trousers. I can't force you to, I can only hope you
understand I'm serious.

(PETROV *and* STAVSKY *come on.* BRIUCHKOV *and* GORKY
behind. GORKY *falls back and goes, leaving* BRIUCHKOV *to
see the* CHEKA *out.*)

ELENA: I'm not going outside tonight. (*Goes.*)

GUMILYOV: Good evening, gentlemen. Have you finished your
business?

PETROV: Very nearly.

GUMILYOV: I think now that the dancing's over, it's time
to go.

PETROV: I think we'd better come with you. It isn't safe outside
and at least we're armed.

GUMILYOV: Are you going my way? I live beyond Morskaya.

PETROV: We can do very easily. If you aren't armed it would be
better if you came with us.

STAVSKY: (*Gently frisking him*) Perhaps he is.
(*Producing the German revolver.*)

GUMILYOV: I use it to wake people up at readings.

PETROV: Come on . . .

GUMILYOV: (*Struggling slightly*) Where are you taking me?

PETROV: Don't let's ruin the party.

(GUMILYOV *collects himself. The men stand aside to let him
leave with dignity.* GUMILYOV *looks over his shoulder to where
sounds of a guitar and laughter are coming. Hoping someone
will appear.*)

GUMILYOV: 'He went off without a word along the shore of the sounding sea.' (*Pause. To them.*) Homer.
(*They go off.* GUMILYOV *screams from off stage* 'Elenotchka!' MAYAKOVSKY *comes in. He looks around then goes to sit down at the table. He takes out his revolver and removes the bullets.* YAGODIN *comes in and starts to play the balalaika to* AVERBACH *and* BRIUCHKOV. MAYAKOVSKY *puts one bullet back in. No one sees. He puts the revolver on to the table, spreads his palms out on the table and stares ahead. He picks up the revolver and spins the chamber. He puts the barrel into his mouth and points it upwards forcing his lips back. He squeezes the trigger. A click. A pause. He takes the gun out of his mouth and puts it away.* LILI *comes back with the two* SAILORS *who are in a bizarre form of evening dress and are wearing theatrical make-up. But they seem too large for their costumes and the effect is grotesque. They are also ill at ease.*)

MAYAKOVSKY: Lelyeckha!

LILI: Volodya! (*She looks at* KUFTIK *who stops and turns round.*) Where have you been?

MAYAKOVSKY: (*Brightly*) Walking! Walking on top of the world! I've missed you!
(GORKY *and the rest of the guests, including* BLOK *come on. Everyone well lubricated.* GORKY *is the centre and everyone groups round him. Only* MAYAKOVSKY *stands aside.*)

GORKY: (*To* BLOK) Your pessimism is just a temporary thing. You glorified the Revolution and you will again. It happens to all of us. (*To* SINGERS.) Comrades, Please! But we have to live *through* these times.

MARINA: Alex . . .
(*Singing fades down.*)

BLOK: But I'm reaching no one, Alex. We're just fooling ourselves if we think we are.

MANDELSTAM: Nobody is listening to us.

GORKY: Millions of people are exhausted after work. Some can't read. Some prefer to sing. Some of them are frightened by us, or don't trust us. Some of them can see that we're scared of them, the great human mass out there. And millions of them have never known the faintest glimmering of enlightenment.

We are really a hateful backward Asia. In the past only a few of those forgotten people ever wormed their way up to the light. Gorky was one of them. Now there will be many, many more.

AVERBACH: There's a tremendous bombardment somewhere.

MANDELSTAM: The guns at Kronstadt, look.

YAGODIN: There's some fighting in the streets, too.

GORKY: What's happening?

NADEZHDA: It's bad for someone, poor souls.

(MARINA *draws* GORKY *aside*.)

MARINA: Alex . . .

(*She takes him upstage and introduces him to the* SAILORS. *Explains what has happened.* GORKY *agitated*.)

BLOK: Strange days . . .

AVERBACH: The rising had to be put down. Some of those boys were led astray. Even a nationalist would draw the line at what the British have been doing.

NADEZHDA: What have they been doing?

AVERBACH: Training party members to be provocateurs. Training them secretly at night in the embassy. This whole strike was a phoney one. It came out of nothing. The Petrograd Soviet has been infiltrated from top to bottom by people on the far left.

MANDELSTAM: Who told you all this?

YAGODIN: It's common knowledge.

AVERBACH: Take a tough line now. It's the only way.

MANDELSTAM: So you mean, the ones who seem to be most militant might be British agents?

AVERBACH: It's quite possible.

MANDELSTAM: So *you* could be one, Leo.

(KUFTIK *laughs*.)

AVERBACH: We're surrounded by cynicism. How many thousands of years must we go on before it's eradicated. It's a disease!

GORKY: Nobody will convince me these sailors are provocateurs . . .

BLOK: They'll surrender quickly. They'll see reason.

NADEZHDA: Listen to those guns. They don't sound very reasonable.

GORKY: They must give them a chance to see reason.

MARINA: They must surrender.

GORKY: These are the proudest men in the world. How can we allow this to happen?

(*Machine gun nearby.*)

GORKY: Where's Volodya?

NADEZHDA: They're getting close.

GORKY: I can't believe that Ilyich can sanction this. I can't believe it of him. (*He looks at* MANDELSTAM.) Osip, why haven't you been to visit me for so long?

MANDELSTAM: You never answered my request, Alex.

GORKY: What request?

MANDELSTAM: About the trousers.

GORKY: Trousers, what trousers?

MANDELSTAM: I applied to you for a pullover and a pair of trousers. Do you remember? But you only sent the pullover.

GORKY: Don't bother me with that now. Dear fellow, don't bother me about your trousers. Borrow some trousers.

(AKHMATOVA *comes on. Goes to* MANDELSTAM.)

AKHMATOVA: Has anyone seen Kolia? Gumilyov . . .

ELENA: He's gone off with another woman. You'll understand, I'm sure.

(GORKY *is centre stage now. The bombardment rises to a crescendo.* GORKY *lets out a howl of despair, like an animal. The lights slowly come down, but before they go out* MAYAKOVSKY *bursts out of the gloom, high above the others.*)

MAYAKOVSKY: Beat on the street the march of rebellion
Soaring above the proud heads of men
We are the flood of a second deluge
Bursting over the world again.

Days are a winged steed
Years drag glum
Our new God is Speed
Our hearts a drum.

Our voices are gold spun
No bullet can sting
Song is our field gun
Gold our throats ring.

Green meadows grow!
Days surge by!
Rainbow arch your bow!
Year horses fly!

(*The lights tighten on* MAYAKOVSKY *highlighting him in a burst of golden colour, like a god.*)

The sky is bored with the stars!
But the songs we sing will survive
So we'll shout to the Great Bear
Hey, you! Lift us to heaven alive!

Sing! Drink sweet.
Veins flow Spring!
Heart beat strong
Breast of brass, ring!

(*Blackout.*)

ACT II

GORKY's apartment again. Great paintings, icons, swathed in cloths and paper, damp and peeling, descend from the flies and settle, making a smaller space. GORKY sits there, gloomy and tired. BRIUCHKOV, YAGODIN. Frozen. MANDELSTAM stands in the room in a spotlight. Speaks ironically, with a smile. Walks through the room.

MANDELSTAM: My brothers let us glorify
  The twilight of freedom
  The great sunset time.
  Into the seething waters of night
  Sinks down a nest of snares.
  Oh sun, judges, people
  You rise up over desolate years!

  Let us glorify the fateful load
  The people's leader bears.
  Let us glorify the dark burden of power
  Its unbearable weight.
  In whom there is a heart
  He must hear the ship of time
  Sink to the bottom of the sea.

  Into militant legions
  We have bound swallows and now
  The sun cannot be seen; the elements
  Lurch, jabber, come alive.
  The earth sails, the sun hides
  Behind dense twilight mists.

  So let us try one vast, awkward
  Rasping turn of the wheel.
  Have courage, friends. The earth is sailing.
  Cleaving the ocean with a plough,
  In bitter Lethean cold, remember
  This earth has cost us tens of heavens.

(*He goes. Lights up.* MARINA *is stirring a foul looking brown potion.* BRIUCHKOV *is dragging in an enormous sack of books, and during the following he and* YAGODIN *empty them out and begin throwing them into a Burzhuyka stove, laughing and calling out the names of the writers at the same time.*)

BRIUCHKOV: Krylov . . . Konevskoy, Fritshe, Sluchevski . . .

GORKY: What disgusting remedy is that?

MARINA: It's made from oak bark to stop your teeth falling out.

(BRIUCHKOV *throws another book into the stove. This produces hysterics in both. More laughter. Three books go in at once.* GORKY *reacts, goes towards the stove,* MARINA *intercepts. Gives him medicine.*)

MARINA: I wish you'd get rid of that little informer.

GORKY: I'm going to reform him. You can help. (*Drinks, grimaces.*) You know the tricks of the trade. Do I have to see anyone else this morning?

MARINA: Alex, I'm sorry darling, I know you're not well . . . but we must try and stick to our routine. There are so many people in the lobby there's a real danger that someone will suffocate.

GORKY: Of course, who's next?

MARINA: There's a pregnant girl outside . . . (*Holds out a thin volume to* GORKY.) . . . she published this when she was fifteen . . . There isn't a man.

GORKY: Yes, yes. Remember her. Is this all there is?

MARINA: She's due in three weeks.

GORKY: Why do they keep on producing babies? In all this! I don't have to see her, do I?

MARINA: Can we make sure she gets a milk ration? She doesn't look very strong.

GORKY: Put her down as Mrs Gorky.

MARINA: (*Resigned*) I can't keep doing that . . .

BRIUCHKOV: Bely . . . Annensky.

GORKY: (*To* BRIUCHKOV) What are you doing? (MARINA *goes.*) Have all the crates gone?

BRIUCHKOV: It's all right. We bought them on the street. Dirt cheap.

GORKY: Did you say Annensky?

YAGODIN: (*Nods*) This is all we could get, apart from white wood which won't burn without choking everyone.

(GORKY *goes over to the stove.*)

GORKY: Did you say Annensky?

(*He picks up some tongs, pokes gently in the fire, fishes out one of the books. He dusts off the scorched cover. Opens the book. He flicks through the pages, touching them gently. Quite a long pause.*)

Mind if I keep this?

BRIUCHKOV: No.

GORKY: Innokenty Annensky. Good poet.

YAGODIN: (*Smiles*) Haven't got anything against him.

GORKY: He's been dead for a few years. (*Leafs through.*) Nineteen nine. (*Mildly.*) Shame to burn him.

(*He puts the book in his pocket.* MARINA *comes in.*)

MARINA: I've just had to get rid of Mandelstam. I didn't think you could cope with him today. He was raving on about some conspiracy against the Acmeists and how he hasn't published any original poetry for some time.

GORKY: Nobody understands a word of it, that's why.

MARINA: But he did say that Kolia Gumilyov's deputy at the academy had been to see him and told him that Gumilyov had gone missing. Almost certainly arrested. He asked you to contact Lenin, because it was urgent and he felt his life was in danger.

GORKY: I don't think his life's in danger for a minute. He's far too well known. Besides, people don't kill poets. (*Laughs.*) They only have to frighten them. We ought to find out if he has been arrested. Someone will tell us soon enough, I suppose. I'm usually the first to hear when anything like that happens.

MARINA: He wants you to ring him back when you've seen Lenin.

GORKY: I've broken with Lenin. Until he explains why they invade my life, why they invade my privacy, why in the name of everything we fought for do they invade my house. This is the way old friends . . .

MARINA: I'm sure you're wrong to take it personally. He can't be responsible for what Petrograd does. You and I know how dangerous the situation is here. That's why so many people are going to Moscow.

GORKY: When they're not going abroad.

MARINA: You should go. Clear up that chest.

GORKY: Never! I've lived with it for fifteen years. It would be misunderstood. Besides, there's so much to be done here. So many millions of spirits to feed. So many out there we must reach, and we will, we will. Just need more time, more resources. Can't keep filling the place with rescued works of art. Got to look after *people*.

MARINA: (*Suddenly upset*) I'd better deal with all these *people* then.

(*She goes.*)

BRIUCHKOV: Alexei Maximovitch, why don't we sell off a couple of these paintings, and buy stuff on the foreign market?

GORKY: I couldn't do that. I'm supposed to be protecting them for the state.

BRIUCHKOV: Do you know how much one of these things would buy?

GORKY: I don't think I *want* to know.

BRIUCHKOV: Market over there's crazy.

GORKY: Capitalism is crazy.

BRIUCHKOV: Government doesn't seem to mind if the odd one gets ripped up by hooligans so why shouldn't you use one to buy essentials? You could get . . . you know, paper, sugar, that sort of thing.

GORKY: Are you trying to say that we should exchange Russian art for things, for capitalist products?

BRIUCHKOV: (*Looking round*) At least they'd be exhibited abroad.

GORKY: How could that be justified morally? How could the government possibly allow that?

BRIUCHKOV: If you ask me, they'd turn a blind eye. Officially.

GORKY: What do you mean?

BRIUCHKOV: The government can't negotiate with certain countries officially.
(GORKY *looks blank*.)
Where have you been for the last few years?
(*He goes back to the stove. Starts to put more books in.* GORKY *stares at* BRIUCHKOV.)

GORKY: Briuchkov, come here. What sort of a writer are you?

BRIUCHKOV: (*Leaving* YAGODIN) I write poetry mostly.

GORKY: Have you anything of yours. That I can read?

BRIUCHKOV: Well no . . . not really. (*Nervous smile*.) Difficult to get hold of any paper. I keep it all in my head.

GORKY: Good, then recite, from your head.
(BRIUCHKOV *takes off a boot which is giving him trouble*.)

GORKY: I know what your game is, you know.

BRIUCHKOV: I thought you did.

GORKY: You don't seem to be making much out of it. I provide you with board and lodgings to spy on me and they give you nothing. So they must be blackmailing you.
(BRIUCHKOV *looks back evenly*.)

GORKY: I can't remember how you first arrived here. One day you just turned up and started doing things. The oh-so-useful Briuchkov. (GORKY *is examining one of* BRIUCHKOV's *ancient boots that he has taken off*.) This is in a terrible state, terrible . . . What we used to do, we used to patch them up with felt (*Demonstrates*.) and fold it double over there and hammer it in with tin tacks along there. Never mind. You're not from round here are you. Why did you come to Petrograd?

BRIUCHKOV: I want to be a poet. I was a clerk for the railway. It was boring. There's nothing much at home . . .

GORKY: You can stay here as long as you like, I won't boot you out. You can tell them anything you like because I'm too well known to touch and they know it. But don't get in any deeper . . .

BRIUCHKOV: Thank you.

GORKY: What did you do? Get caught thieving? They shoot you for that, don't they? They can make you do anything, can't they?

58

(BRIUCHKOV *looks back evenly.* MARINA *comes on with* BLOK.)

MARINA: Alex . . .

GORKY: Make him out an order for some boots . . . and some paper.

(BLOK *is standing upstage in the shadows.* MARINA *indicates this with a look.* BLOK *comes forward, diffidently.*
BRIUCHKOV *goes back to join* YAGODIN *at the stove.*
YAGODIN *has been reading.* BRIUCHKOV *takes the book, throws it in.*)

BLOK: Alex . . .

GORKY: Blok, my dear fellow.

BLOK: Alex, I'm sorry to trouble you. To burst in on you like this . . .

(BLOK *stands, out of breath, for a few moments.*)

GORKY: My dear chap, what is it?

BLOK: I know you have your own troubles. (*Pause.*) Mine . . . I've applied for permission to leave the country, three times . . . in fact. Been refused every time. Can't understand it.

GORKY: (*Stunned*) Why?

BLOK: No idea. They won't say.

GORKY: Why do you want to leave? The loss of someone of your stature would be a terrible blow to us . . . I thought you of all people . . .

BLOK: It's simply a question . . . of health. Everyone has done their best for me. But . . . my asthma is now very severe and they've put us, for the best of all possible reasons I'm sure, in a centrally heated apartment . . . which is impossible for my breathing . . . besides which the cold generally . . . It seems that nothing we do – gets through. Treated with suspicion. Would only want to winter abroad if permission were granted. Get better. Come back again soon.

GORKY: Of course, of course. I understand. It's a difficult situation. Your poetry gave us so much inspiration in the early days. No one welcomed the Revolution with such intensity.

BLOK: I seem to have cooled off a bit. That it? Yes. It's true. But not, fatal . . . Difficult times to explain, Alex.

GORKY: Where do you . . . stand now?

BLOK: I'm not one of those intellectuals of the old school . . . who moan on about their loss of rights and how the 'secret power' has shut down their crumbling organizations and their newspapers, most of which were appalling anyway . . .

GORKY: We've been unlucky. Not one country on earth has given us a leg up. And now this famine . . . I'm sorry. What do you want me to do?

BLOK: I wonder if you could . . . perhaps mention it to Lenin. (*A pause.* MARINA *comes on, waits, noticing the atmosphere.*) Not to be alarmist. But now . . . feel sure it's a matter of life and . . .

GORKY: Yes, yes . . . I'll do my best.

MARINA: Akhmatova is here. About Gumilyov.

GORKY: Tell her I'm busy. Tell her to get me facts. Where he is. Why he's been arrested. Facts.
(*The* GORKY *set trucks back, the pictures go.* BRIUCHKOV *is left on stage, about to read a statement. Spot follows* AVERBACH.)

AVERBACH: Comrades . . . We the Russian Association of Proletcultist writers would like to welcome Symbolists, Futurists, Acmeists, all literary groups, to their meeting. (*The cast appear from all sides to take up their places in a meeting at the Stray Dog. They are all smoking intensely and there is soon a heavy pall of smoke in the air.* MANDELSTAM MAYAKOVSKY, LILI, TUMIN, YAGODIN, BRIUCHKOV, KUFTIK, NADEZHDA. FUTURISTS *and* PROLETCULT *on opposite sides.*)

AVERBACH: Now. Where shall we begin?

BRIUCHKOV: Comrades . . .
(MAYAKOVSKY *stands, suddenly.*)

MAYAKOVSKY: Comrades, I want to stand up and walk around then I don't have to think I'm in a meeting.

AVERBACH: (*Smiling*) Thank you. I think comrade Mayakovsky meant this as a graphic demonstration of the content of our meeting. The individual against the collective. Shall we call it that?

MAYAKOVSKY: I don't mind what you call it. But for heaven's sake put some life into it.

AVERBACH: (*Pauses, inclines his head*) The events of the past few days have taught us artists a lesson. Don't be complacent. There's an enemy within the country and an enemy within ourselves. Some of our best-loved writers are throwing up their hands and saying 'Oh dear, the Bolsheviks didn't ought to do this!' and 'We thought they were humane!' and so on. All those who prefer the Revolution to be a fantasy and don't much like the reality when it comes along. And we know what happens to them.

BRIUCHKOV: Yes. I want to . . .

AVERBACH: One minute. Unless we put ourselves unequivocally on the side of the proletariat, history is just going to give us a quick elbow in the ribs and shove us out of the way. We have to let go of our old selves. The Revolution has made bourgeois culture impossible. There's no longer a bourgeoisie to enjoy it. They're all in Paris! (*Some laughter.*) Who have they left us? Not much. A few low priests of high art. A bit threadbare now. (*This becomes more and more pointed towards* MANDELSTAM.) These people who didn't have the guts to emigrate. Only their souls have emigrated. Internal *émigrés*. Misfits. Bohemian drop-outs, bewailing the so-called glories of the past that ordinary Russians never glimpsed. They made the models for literary society. But unfortunately some of our most useful writers are hopelessly addicted, like morphine addicts. Literary groups . . . (*Pause.*) I propose the end of literary groups. We must be part of one movement, a historically inevitable movement. We must speak a common language and it must be the language of the people. We must tell them stories they understand. We must listen to their stories because believe me there are many of them. We must take our simple offerings to every corner of the Soviet Union, not sit in tiny rooms and listen to the spoilt Bohemian nonsense of the disenchanted. We know that the party will eventually put its full weight behind our movement. I know this because although I don't have a private telephone to the Kremlin, this is the inevitable consequence of foreseeable events. This is why you must accept our generosity and goodwill. This is why, comrades, we want to win the best of you to our side.

(LILI *stands up eagerly.*)

LILI: We've been hearing all this crap about Futurism being dead for a long time. Our movement still seems to be alive. Perhaps it's the name that worries you? We stick with the name of Futurism because it's the name that is still well known enough for people to rally to. When the masses understand the term as we understand it, then perhaps we shall call it something else. For about a year we've had to put up with the most boring kind of logic and attempts to prove various minnow-sized truths like the ones we've just been listening to. Let me remind you of the principles on which our 'salon' was based and leave you with those to contemplate. To crush the ecumenical frost which turned inspiration into ice! To throw all the so-called great names of literature off the boat! And to destroy the old language which was too senile to keep pace with the speed of modern life! We have almost finished this task and just as we're beginning to construct something noble in the spirit of the new man, we're told that we are no longer relevant . . . by people, these imperialists of culture, who have been conspicuous by their absence when all the demolition work was being done. It all seems very suspicious to me.

AVERBACH: Nobody is belittling the extraordinary work that was done. Perhaps I should put my remarks in a more dialectical way; we are talking about a progressive literature . . .

BRIUCHKOV: Comrades, I have something important to say . . .

MANDELSTAM: The theory of progress is suicidal! All it means is that writers are so busy trying to clear a path for their successors that they can't even accomplish their own tasks. It sounds like some competition for the improvement of a machine except that nobody knows where the judges are or what the machine is for. What we have here (*Points at* AVERBACH.) is collectivism without the collective. We're now all of us on one side or the other of a divided truth. All the patents have been filed and we're not expecting any new ones for a long time. All I know is that if you cut poetry off from the past, if you pretend it has never had one, and if you take out everything that's remotely ambiguous, what you produce may be all very well but it won't be poetry. For God's sake let's educate the masses so they can appreciate the real thing even if we don't agree what the real thing is. But don't let's feed them pap before they can read. I wonder if our poor uneducated people realize that folklore is about to descend on them like a voracious caterpillar. Anyway there are far too many poets and not enough readers. As for the snide character assassination that was embedded in your critical thuggery, I'll ignore it. I'm just relieved that in this desperate bid to give credibility to your movement it is Mayakovsky and not Mandelstam that you want to seduce.

(*Some uncomfortable stirring.* AVERBACH *looks angry.*)

MAYAKOVSKY: My colleague Lili Brik was wrong. The Futurists are dead. Before the Revolution we were all stormy youth and rebellion. Our manifestos used to demand the destruction of privilege. What are they doing now? Checking authors for the right credentials. We used to rebel against traditional clothes and wear yellow jackets, now we find we're wearing the cast-off coats of the poorest peasantry in our glorious inverted snobbery. The Golden Future is near enough to touch. And the Futurists look like becoming the Presentists. That is what this meeting is really about. The Futurists created style. The Presentists only follow it. (*Pointing to* AVERBACH.) This man is the high priest of the Presentists. If we join him we are already lowering our sights. Our lives pass so quickly. We are

growing old. So let's bury Futurism. No, we won't join
you, Leo. We have just created LEF! The Left Front of
Art! A new literary group. We shall continue to write
whatever we please, wear whatever we please, appear
wherever we please and do exactly *as* we please! (*Lowers his
voice.*) In this way we will continue to build a new art for
the Soviet Union.

(MAYAKOVSKY *makes for the exit.* AVERBACH *stands, quite
calm.*)

AVERBACH: If you put yourself so unequivocally at the disposal
of the Soviet Union, perhaps you'll show everybody your
party card.

MAYAKOVSKY: I'm a poet, not a politician. I don't need to
prove my commitment to the Revolution. My life speaks for
itself.

BRIK: How can you stand beside this man and claim . . .

AVERBACH: I'm not claiming anything as an individual. We will
just have to let the movement express itself collectively on
the subject of comrade Mayakovsky's individual status.
Perhaps when you see the way things are moving, you'll
reconsider your position.

(MAYAKOVSKY *goes.* AVERBACH *and* YAGODIN *stand up to
leave.* BRIUCHKOV *finally holds the floor.*)

BRIUCHKOV: You've all forgotten where the roots are. The
roots. What we need in Russia is a true Dionysian state
. . . a sort of synthesis of Christianity and the pagan
religions.

(*The lights change and the others freeze, then fade away. We
are in* AKHMATOVA's *apartment. Bare room.*)

Do you believe there's still a God? I'd like to see orchestras
everywhere and regular feast days for the people . . . mass
dancing choruses, revive tragedy again, not the Greek sort,
but real Russian myths. Beautiful maidens in the villages,
their hair garlanded in flowers . . .

AKHMATOVA: Vladimir and Eurydice.

BRIUCHKOV: Isn't it wonderful? My favourite one.

AKHMATOVA: Wonderful. (*Studies him.*) That's a very
interesting idea. I wonder where it came from.

BRIUCHKOV: Do you think there's a God?

AKHMATOVA: Ah. Sometimes. And then sometimes not.

BRIUCHKOV: I do. Despite all the pain and suffering in our poor impoverished land. The whole problem is to reconcile this with Marxism. In my worst moments I imagine us completely cut off from the past, completely isolated from world culture. Doesn't it worry you?

AKHMATOVA: I never worry about the future.

BRIUCHKOV: You seem to be worried about something.

AKHMATOVA: Yes, I'm very worried about a friend of mine who is missing. I'm expecting a telephone call.

BRIUCHKOV: Might I inquire who?

AKHMATOVA: I'm sorry I haven't anything to offer you. You caught me by surprise.

BRIUCHKOV: Aha! (*Looks round.*) It's rather a bare apartment now, isn't it? (*Pause.*) Have you ever thought of emigrating?

AKHMATOVA: No. Never.

BRIUCHKOV: I'm told the theatre's very good in New York.

AKHMATOVA: So I've heard.

BRIUCHKOV: I wish I had your power. To be the most widely-read poet in the whole of Russia. Ah, me!

AKHMATOVA: I don't feel I have any power.

BRIUCHKOV: You do. I assure you, you do.

AKHMATOVA: You make me sound like a witch doctor.

BRIUCHKOV: This may sound rather impertinent but would you read to me?

AKHMATOVA: I'm sorry. It isn't the right time, is it? (*Pause*) But please leave your verses with me. You have brought them?

BRIUCHKOV: (*A slight pause.*) I've been thinking. I rather need to correct them before I take such a terrifying step. I'm really rather nervous about showing them to you. Could I bring them back to you another time?

AKHMATOVA: But I thought that was why you came.

BRIUCHKOV: (*Going to the crucifix*) I'm always drawn to this. It was Gumilyov who gave it to you, wasn't it? (*Caressing it.*) Didn't you tell me? Beautiful.

(AKHMATOVA *holds a hand to her face. A quick glance at the telephone.*)

AKHMATOVA: (*Sharply*) What was the purpose of this visit?

BRIUCHKOV: (*Caught off-guard*) Well . . . as I said . . . I'm one of your greatest admirers . . . more than that, I . . .

AKHMATOVA: You're a very bad liar.

BRIUCHKOV: I'm in love with you.

AKHMATOVA: You're not in love with me.

BRIUCHKOV: I am, please, believe me.

AKHMATOVA: At first I thought you'd come to borrow money.

BRIUCHKOV: (*Grasping at a straw*) I'm sorry . . . Times are very hard.

AKHMATOVA: You can keep this. I hope it brings you luck. (*She hands him the crucifix.*)

BRIUCHKOV: Anna Andreyevna . . .

AKHMATOVA: Please go.

BRIUCHKOV: (*With sudden intensity*) Believe me.

AKHMATOVA: You're some sort of an informer. What do you want? You probably don't even know yourself, you wretched creature. What do you want, some sort of personal statement to put in a file? Is this all connected with Gumilyov? If you know anything about this . . . Where is Kolia? Do you know where he is?

BRIUCHKOV: (*Dejected*) I don't know. I hope that you know how to survive. If I can . . . help in any way. (*With sudden sincerity.*) I would go through hell for . . .

AKHMATOVA: I'll survive. I'll even survive intrusions on my privacy. If you believe all that nonsense about spiritual power I'm very sorry for you. But I'm even more sorry for you if you looked it up in a book which I strongly suspect is what you did do. Now then . . . my attitude to the past? I don't have an ounce of nostalgia in me. The wonderful thing about the future is it always recedes, particularly when it promises happiness. I welcome the Revolution . . . yes, I do because I don't need happiness. Going without food is irrelevant. I've starved clinically twice since the Revolution. And look at me, I'm not a ghost, am I? I'm a survivor. What else do you want to know? I like to get

66

drunk occasionally. My favourite politician? Garibaldi. A revolutionary himself. My least favourite writer? Tolstoy. You see, I'm an inexhaustible supply of heresies. I enjoy being made to laugh unexpectedly, as I have been doing continually since you arrived. I'm looking for a new lover. But I still love Kolia. My favourite colour is purple . . . but it has no . . . episcopal significance.

BRIUCHKOV: (*Stunned*) Please forgive me.

AKHMATOVA: Tell them from me. Kolia's a brilliant fool. He talks too much. He's a fantasist. Nothing he says is real . . .

BRIUCHKOV: It is . . . very hard to make a living. Please forgive me.

AKHMATOVA: I'm sure. (*With a little irony.*) You are forgiven. Make sure the door to the street is closed when you go out.

(BRIUCHKOV *goes out, still clutching the crucifix.*

AKHMATOVA *goes to the phone.*

PETROV *and* GUMILYOV *come up from below.* CHEKA *headquarters.* PETROV *throws a leaflet on the table.*)

PETROV: Do you recognize this?

(GUMILYOV *tries to look at it without moving.*)

GUMILYOV: No.

PETROV: (*Unruffled*) Look at it carefully.

(GUMILYOV *exhales. Picks it up grudgingly. Pause.*)

GUMILYOV: I'd say it was anti-Bolshevik propaganda.

PETROV: Did you write it?

GUMILYOV: No! (*Angrily*) Absolutely not.

PETROV: I'd say it was written by someone who knew how to write.

GUMILYOV: Most things are.

(PETROV *smiles bleakly.*)

It's absurd. Cloak-and-dagger stuff.

PETROV: Do you agree with any of the sentiments expressed in it?

GUMILYOV: Not if they're put like that.

(GUMILYOV *drops the leaflet on the desk. Pause.*)

PETROV: Do you know Professor Tagentsev?

GUMILYOV: Of course. Who doesn't?

PETROV: Is he the kind of man to be mixed up in this?

GUMILYOV: Mixed up in what?

PETROV: This anti-Bolshevik conspiracy.

GUMILYOV: I've never discussed politics with him.

PETRON: Can you remember where you were on the eighth of this month between eight and midnight?

GUMILYOV: (*After a pause*) Yes, I was reading my poetry, at the Free Trade Hall on Morskaya.

(PETROV *writes a note.*)

PETROV: So there are people who can back this up?

GUMILYOV: There were about two thousand people there. I think they noticed me.

PETROV: How long were you there?

GUMILYOV: Past midnight. How long are you keeping me here?

PETROV: Until I find out if you're telling the truth.

GUMILYOV: Does it matter to you?

PETROV: It does. To me. (*He shuffles his papers together.*)

GUMILYOV: I'd like a copy of the *Iliad* and the Bible if I'm going to be kept waiting.

(PETROV *looks at* GUMILYOV *carefully.*)

Nobody knows I'm here. I do have friends. They'll miss me.

PETROV: Was it so unexpected? Unfortunately I haven't been given permission to tell anyone your whereabouts. Other enquiries are being made, about other people. So, I'm afraid you're going to have to wait a little while longer.

GUMILYOV: Please, please. Don't even apologize. Historically I'm in good company . . . Dostoevsky, Pushkin.

PETROV: I'd say you've been in pretty bad company.

GUMILYOV: You've heard of Pushkin, have you?

PETROV: (*Stiff, offended*) Of course.

GUMILYOV: Oh, of course, we're a great nation of poetry lovers. It's true you don't seem to have hairs on the palms of your hands. What are you doing in the Cheka if you've heard of Pushkin?

(PETROV *doesn't respond immediately. Aware that* GUMILYOV *may not be worth the response.*)

PETROV: I was a lieutenant in the Red Army. My regiment took heavy casualties in the Ukraine at the end of the war. We were disbanded. (*Pause.*) It's a job. (*Correcting himself.*) An important job.

GUMILYOV: Do you know how Pushkin died?

PETROV: After a duel.

GUMILYOV: Yes! But more subtle than that. The Tsar's secret police tricked him into a duel they knew he'd lose. What do you think of that?

PETROV: Barbaric. (*Without irony.*) What a waste.

GUMILYOV: Without a doubt.

PETROV: But then Russian poets have tended to be self-destructive, have they not?

(*The two men observe each other, not unfriendly.*)

GUMILYOV: Have you ever read my poetry?

PETROV: I'm afraid not.

(GUMILYOV *produces a small, exquisitely bound book.*)

GUMILYOV: It seems rather arrogant of me to carry them around with me, but I thought . . . in case I was here for any length of time.

(GUMILYOV *smiles cheekily.* PETROV *reaches out for the book. A pause.* PETROV *leafs through book.*)

PETROV: You had time to prepare yourself then.

GUMILYOV: Do you read poetry?

PETROV: Yes. When we were fighting the Germans in the trenches. I liked . . . what was her name? 'How past mending my heart was frozen, yet the tread of my feet was light. For my left I found I had chosen . . . the glove that belonged to the right.' She was very popular in the war. Akhmatova . . .

(GUMILYOV *laughs.*)

You don't like her stuff? She wrote about lovers and parting and the pain of it, the cruelty. So much of it in the world . . .

GUMILYOV: I knew her well . . .

PETROV: (*Genuine embarrassment*) She's dead?

GUMILYOV: No. We were married . . .

PETROV: I didn't know that.

GUMILYOV: We don't want to talk about my private life, do we?

PETROV: You want something to read?

(He reaches in the desk drawer and produces a manuscript.)
This is something I wrote when I was in the army.
Descriptions of army life and records of battles and
engagements. My own thoughts, characters I met. I'd like
to have your opinion of them. Your honest opinion. Don't
pull any punches.

GUMILYOV: I've never given criticism under quite these
conditions before.

PETROV: On the other hand don't be too hard on them. I've
never shown them to anyone before.

(GUMILYOV laughs. Takes the file.)
It's my first attempt.

GUMILYOV: I shall be honest.

PETROV: I hope so. *(Calls out.)* Talberg!

(A young CHEKA man comes in.)
Make sure this man has a more comfortable chair and a
reading light.

*(He goes out. Fade on GUMILYOV as he opens the
manuscript.*
The club. TUMIN, MANDELSTAM, NADEZHDA, KUFTIK.)

KUFTIK: *(Cynically)* This is the Stray Dog Café
Poets and painters at play
The Revolution
Is almost won
In Petrograd
It's fun it's fun it's fun
In Petrograd.

TUMIN: Where are all my brave Futurists? Look at us! We're
nothing. Nothingists.

MANDELSTAM: Did you take a message for me?

TUMIN: I can't remember everyone who telephones.

MANDELSTAM: You're lying. Why didn't you pass the message
on?

TUMIN: Poets are always quarrelling. How do I know you and
Gumilyov are even on speaking terms?

MANDELSTAM: Would it matter, in the situation he's in?
(MANDELSTAM goes to another table.)

TUMIN: *(To NADEZHDA)* Nadia dear, you're not going to make

any trouble? You know what a hard time we've been having recently. We've absolutely no idea what he's been up to. He might be guilty of some crime.

NADEZHDA: What does it matter? He's a poet. You make your living out of them. We can't allow him to be locked up without a fair trial.

TUMIN: We're little people. We can't get mixed up in politics.

NADEZHDA: It's very strange but I've noticed that people I knew before the Revolution have started to hide behind a kind of mask.

TUMIN: You're very young and very naïve. But please do whatever you have to do somewhere else. I've let you hang around here because you've got nowhere else to go.

NADEZHDA: It's as if the expressions we used to wear have become frozen. It's very unnerving. We're becoming caricatures of ourselves.

TUMIN: I always thought your greatest strength, Nadia, was that you said very little. It's obvious to me now that you said very little because you knew very little.

MANDELSTAM: . . . Ladies and gentlemen, I have a petition . . .

(TUMIN *sees* MANDELSTAM *has a petition.*)

TUMIN: No. I can't allow it.

MANDELSTAM: We can't wait for Gorky.

TUMIN: If Gorky says he'll do something, he'll do something.

MANDELSTAM: I'm still waiting for a new pair of trousers.

TUMIN: Gumilyov's a white, in everything but name.

MANDELSTAM: You boil on the face of humanity. (*He points his umbrella at* TUMIN'*s throat.*) You are a lazy, greedy functionary with the backbone of a squid. You're only concerned about the small stock of delicacies you keep hidden in the safe in your office and out of which I expect you're making a fat profit.

TUMIN: I suppose you haven't heard? There's a new Economic Policy. It's legal. I only keep them in the safe to stop the boys stealing them. (*To* MANDELSTAM.) I don't want you here. Or any of your group. Akhmatova, or Gumilyov or any of your gang. You're bad luck. You belong to the past.

The past is over.

(ELENA *comes in. Drops a bag on the floor. Tries to get out without being seen.* MANDELSTAM *has recognized* ELENA *and goes over to her table.*)

MANDELSTAM: You were with Gumilyov the other night. Do you know what happened to him?

ELENA: No.

TUMIN: (*To* MANDELSTAM) I suppose you realize he might be involved in an anti-Bolshevik conspiracy?

NADEZHDA: We're asking for his release pending a fair trial.

MANDELSTAM: Do you know where they took him?

ELENA: I can't talk about it. There's nothing I can do to help.

TUMIN: Why don't you leave her alone? She's frightened.

ELENA: It's all right. (*She fumbles in her hold-all and takes out a pair of trousers.*) He said I was to give you these. I don't know where he is. I swear it.

(*She goes.* MAYAKOVSKY *and* LILI *come in.*)

MANDELSTAM: Did you know Gumilyov's been arrested?

MAYAKOVSKY: (*Taken aback*) I didn't. No.

TUMIN: It's all rumour and hearsay.

NADEZHDA: It's important that we have some information about him. Will you sign this petition?

TUMIN: You have no conception of how careful I have to be. (*To* MAYAKOVSKY.) Do you know anything about this?

MAYAKOVSKY: I know Kolia, I'm afraid. What's he been arrested for?

MANDELSTAM: Some sort of misdemeanour at his official post.

MAYAKOVSKY: That doesn't sound too serious. He'll be all right.

MANDELSTAM: He doesn't have an official post!

NADEZHDA: (*To* MAYAKOVSKY) Will you sign?

MAYAKOVSKY: (*Handing back the petition*) Kolia . . . is a difficult man. He and I, you and I . . . we're on different sides. I don't know . . . Get on to Gorky. Phone him and keep phoning.

(*Suddenly the stage is full as the* PROLETCULT *streams in. They go 'backstage'.* TUMIN *agitated,* YAGODIN *stands up.*)

AVERBACH: Where is Mayakovsky? I've come to see the 'Poet of the Revolution'.

TUMIN: What do you want with him?

YAGODIN: No . . . it's just . . . I didn't understand a word he said last time.

TUMIN: You might be disappointed.

YAGODIN: What's the matter?

TUMIN: He's deserted poetry for the cinema.

YAGODIN: Oh dear, not again. That same old eternal triangle. Moons and flaming Junes.

TUMIN: Briuchkov!

YAGODIN: (*Shouting across to* BRIUCHKOV) Hey, Briuchkov. You look as if you need a good square meal. Get down to the Proletcult Theatre. They want a dozen set painters overnight and as much kasha as you can eat. You don't want to hang around here, they're bad for your health these places.

(BRIUCHKOV *threads his way through the mêlée to read. He is tripped up. Gets there in the end.* KUFTIK *closes.*)

BRIUCHKOV: (*Reciting*) I am the colour of the New Age
No longer brittle
Like the dried pips
Of an orange
Setting in splendour
In the nocturne sky
But the stately blue tips
Of a steel-grey pylon.

I am the sound of the New Age . . .

(BRIUCHKOV *is drowned out and eventually pulled off the stage.* KUFTIK *holds the floor again, flashing his gloves and black lipstick, playing silent-cinema music.* AVERBACH *gets up, with attaché case.*)

AVERBACH: I'm now going to read something a bit more useful. A bit more factual. It's a short story. Don't worry, it isn't very long. (*To* KUFTIK *who is still playing.*) Shut up. (*Pause.*) You effeminate weasel. 'The sudden cold detained the partisans in the Tungus encampment for two days. The cold had been brought in by the ice floes which the wind had driven along from the misty Shantar Islands. So cold

was it . . .' (*A chorus of mocking 'Oooohs!' from the Futurists.*
AVERBACH *looks steely.*) '. . . so very, very bitter that
despite it being very nearly the month of June . . . the
partisans froze at night by their meagre camp fires, whilst
the Tungust slept in bags of reindeer skin. The old fellers
were saying there wouldn't be any fish that year and sure
enough the ice repelled those magnificent humped-backed
salmon . . .'

KUFTIK: Sheep shit!

(*Some laughter.* AVERBACH *makes a sign to* YAGODIN, *and
steps down.* YAGODIN *gets up. A hush.*)

TUMIN: Mayakovsky!

(*A ballerina appears, dancing. It is* LILI *wearing the stylized
make-up of the early cinema. She dances in a spot.*
MAYAKOVSKY *comes on dressed in an extraordinary way; his
hair a romantic lick, his clothes are extravagant and he is
sporting a floppy 'painter's' silk tie.* LILI *strikes a pose. Music.
Strobe light. They dance brilliantly.*)

MAYAKOVSKY: The painter Ivan Nov has fallen for the
ballet-dancer Heart-of-the-Screen in the film *Heart of the
Screen*. Applauding alone in the darkened cinema . . .
(MAYAKOVSKY *begins to strike poses like an actor in the silent
cinema.*)

LILI: . . . He is amazed when she steps out of the screen.

MAYAKOVSKY: He tries to take her home.

LILI: (*Posing*) But she isn't happy in the streets and disappears
through the locked door of the cinema.

MAYAKOVSKY: The painter falls ill . . .

LILI: He is brought a poster of the film. He hangs it on the wall.
The ballet dancer comes to life.

MAYAKOVSKY: The painter persuades the ballet dancer to live
with him. She pines for the screen. She throws herself at
everything white . . .
(LILI *throws herself around the room.*)
She escapes and ends up in a café which is frequented by
poets and painters.

LILI: There she meets a gypsy girl in love with the painter. The
gypsy girl stabs her through the heart.

74

MAYAKOVSKY: The painter walking home that night sees a poster for the film . . . which shows a knife through the dancer's heart . . . He studies the poster for a clue. He sees the name of film land . . . and resolves to travel there to find his love.

(PROLETCULTIST *catcalls*.)

All right, he flushes his decadent painter's clothes down the toilet, puts on a cap and dungarees, borrows his father's leather jacket and talks in a really rough voice so he doesn't looks like a big daisy.

(*Anger from the* PROLETCULT.)

YAGODIN: What is this place? Russia? Or a brothel in Montmartre? (*Looks around him, indicating all the murals*.) Look comrades, the future! Where do you get the impression from that you're the Poet of the Revolution, Mayakovsky?

MAYAKOVSKY: From the place dialectically opposed to where the question was born. (*Laughter*.)

PROLETCULTIST: Mayakovsky, we've heard you're a proletarian poet collectivist. Is that right?

MAYAKOVSKY: If you say so, I'm a proletarian poet collectivist.

PROLETCULTIST: Then why are you always writing I,I,I,?

MAYAKOVSKY: So what was Nicholas the Second? Was he a proletarian poet collectivist? He was always writing we, we, we!

AVERBACH: All this shit is finished. The workers need revolutionary energy.

MANDELSTAM: Stop. All this is irrelevant. I'm talking about the fate of a fellow artist. It's important that every writer demands the release of Gumilyov pending a fair trial.

AVERBACH: The Proletcult will write on any theme!

MAYAKOVSKY: Any theme from Kulaks to cat furs in the state trading store.

(MAYAKOVSKY *hurls a chair upstage*.)

AVERBACH: I'll tell you what the Proletcult is all about . . .

MAYAKOVSKY: No, I'll tell you what the Proletcult is all about. You spend all day at some factory or other and get in everybody's way and then get your hair caught in the machinery and write a lot of badger's droppings called poetry, about not leaving nails lying around on staircases.

PROLETCULTIST: So you refuse to write poetry of the Revolution, comrade?

YAGODIN: Have you noticed how all the heroes in the murals look like the Poet of the Revolution? Muscle bound!

AVERBACH: Listen, comrade, this is getting out of hand. Why don't we go somewhere and talk things through rationally? All these contradictions can be resolved.

YAGODIN: Nobody could accuse the Poet of the Revolution of being a petit bourgeois individualist, could they? Look! He's gone back to wearing make-up. He doesn't want people to take him seriously.

(MAYAKOVSKY *hits* YAGODIN. *General fight.*)

TUMIN: Why are you doing this? This is my club! It's mine! Mine! Mine! Stop!

(*The club is destroyed. Through the debris and the smoke, a familiar bald figure.*)

LENIN: (*Evenly*) The party supports no group in preference to another. We only ask artists to support the Revolution in spirit. We can't build a new culture overnight. It's always good to have a struggle. That's how everything gets resolved in the end.

(LENIN *walks through the chaos quite unconcerned. The club lights dim and the music is harsh and discordant. We are in Lenin's study at the Kremlin. He and* GORKY *are in the middle of a blazing row.*)

I'll give you a permit for Blok to leave as a gesture of trust because of an old and close friendship between us. But it's the last time. This situation with individuals has happened again and again. As far as I can tell you've practically lived on the train between here and Petrograd. The wires that have passed between us would have kept a small telegraph company in business for a year. All about some individual or other . . . And in most cases, because of our old friendship or where justice demanded it, I have managed to fulfil this function you ask of me, and run the country as well! But this has to be the last time.

76

GORKY: Let them die. Shoot them down like the thousands of sailors at Kronstadt.

LENIN: If they are our enemies, yes.

GORKY: Innocent people are being shot all the time. The Cheka practically live in my house.

LENIN: I can't control everything the Petrograd Cheka does.

GORKY: How many nights have you stayed in my house?
(LENIN *is affected by this. A pause.*)

LENIN: Quite often, yes. But in the past. In Capri. It was all theory and chess then.

GORKY: To threaten a man with death for being what he is is absolute proof of moral impotence.

LENIN: (*Exasperated*) Alex, this is not Capri! There has been a revolution and you and the Kronstadt sailors and the bloody intellectuals must learn there is no third way that doesn't end with thousands of workers on the end of foreign and Tsarist bayonets.
(LENIN *comes downstage and sits in the armchair. Stretches out, almost horizontally.*)

GORKY: I want nothing more, Ilyich, than to be the loyal servant of a humanitarian socialist state.

LENIN: The Revolution isn't a magic talisman. We can't conjure up harmony by waving a magic wand in the forest. We are always going to disappoint you, Alex. Are you for us or agin us?

GORKY: (*Sitting down, mumbling*) For, for . . .

LENIN: (*After a pause*) Are you taking care of yourself?
(GORKY *waves this away.*)
Look at you. You've been here half an hour and you're still out of breath from climbing the stairs. Are you spitting blood? You should go to a good sanatorium in Europe and get it cleared up.

GORKY: Please don't ask me to go away. I'm not an *émigré*.

LENIN: Are you doing any writing?

GORKY: I wish I was.

LENIN: Of course you're not. Too many wretched intellectuals to wet-nurse. Take some time off, they can look after themselves for a while. Let Darwin take his course.

(*Laughs*.) Survival of the fittest.

(GORKY *is offended by this and stands up, ready to leave*.)

GORKY: Ilyich . . .

LENIN: (*Motioning him to sit down again*) When are you going to give us another book like *The Mother*?

GORKY: It's a mess. Goes on for ever.

LENIN: (*Simply*) If I'd had the choice of another life I would have been a novelist and I would have written *The Mother*. (*Another pause*.) Tell me, what do you think of Mayakovsky? I didn't like the look of him for a while. You know I have rather conservative tastes, I couldn't understand why the words jumped across the page, but I saw him talk to some foundry workers in the city. It was astonishing. They genuinely loved the man. What riches . . . we have Gorky and we have Mayakovsky.

GORKY: It must have been the first cultural event you've been to since you took me to the music hall in London.

LENIN: (*Sleepily*) The music hall. What was it called?

GORKY: Wilton's. You told us it was a 'small democratic theatre'.

LENIN: Did I? I don't remember that.

GORKY: I remember making a note in my diary that you laughed at the clowns.

LENIN: They were good . . . a little eccentric. (*Looks sharply at him*.) Were you taking notes? I could never get that tune out of my head. For years. What was it?

(*He starts to hum, tunelessly, then tails off.* GORKY *sits stiffly. He realizes that* LENIN *is asleep. He softens slightly, sits watching him.* LENIN *wakes up, almost imperceptibly*.)

I remember at one point in the evening the stage was turned into a lumber yard. These two chaps, supposedly from British Colombia, demolished a huge tree (*Gestures*.) wide as this, in about two minutes flat. Do you remember? Obviously the part of the tree that we couldn't see had been sawn through before the performance. It was an obvious confidence trick. (*Pause*.) I think perhaps at that moment I got closest to understanding why capitalism is still so attractive to the British working class.

78

GORKY: (*Standing suddenly*) Ilyich. I was utterly devastated by the events of this winter at Kronstadt. I couldn't sleep. I became very ill. I was particularly disturbed by the suggestion that these workers, these sailors, were enemies . . . provocateurs. I felt it very deeply and bitterly. I abhor the appalling bloodshed.

LENIN: It is time for you to know that politics is in general a dirty business. It would be much better for you if you don't get mixed up in it any more. Look at me! I'm so tired that I can't do the tiniest little thing. And you're spitting blood and you don't leave! Go to Europe, to a good sanatorium. Cure yourself and do three times as many big things. In Russia there's only busy-body work for you at the moment. And *futile, senseless trivialities*.

GORKY: Is this . . . a banishment?

LENIN: No! Well, all right, in a friendly way. Yes. For your own good.

GORKY: Can I have your promise that Blok . . .

LENIN: This is the last time. I can't give you my promise about that kind of thing any more. (*He stands.*) I'll see you out.

GORKY: (*Confused*) There was someone else . . . No.

(*He is already on his way to the door.* LENIN *follows him, solicitously. He begins to hum the tune of 'Lily of Laguna', pleased that he's remembered it. They shake hands at the door. An air of finality. Something is mumbled.* GORKY *walks downstage, putting on a Chinese dressing-gown and fez; the effect is bizarre. He settles on a couch, dozing, with a thermometer in his mouth as* LENIN *exits, singing confidently.*)

LENIN: 'I *know* she likes me,
I know she likes me . . .
Because she *said* so.

She is my lily of Laguna
She is my lily
And my rose.'

(*Lights up on* GUMILYOV. *He is leaning forward, taunting a silent* CHEKA *man.*)

79

GUMILYOV: I expect you're getting pretty jumpy. All those loyal
sailors suddenly turning against you. Look, it's been three
days . . . it seems like three days. I haven't heard a bird or
seen an inch of sky. What happened to the comrade who I
spoke to first? Our friend the writer. I never saw him again.
He just left me this manuscript . . . if you're going to keep
me here you could at least find me something to read . . .
(*The* CHEKA *man is impassive.*) I wish I'd heard about this
conspiracy from somewhere else. I would have liked to be
involved . . . I suppose that's guilt enough nowadays. I went
to a couple of meetings. I am a monarchist . . . (*Pause.*) I'd
like to see the Romanovs come riding back into Petersburg
on ghostly white horses with flaming swords and drive you
all into the Baltic. (*No response.*) Why do you think he never
came back? Do you think he was afraid of what I was going
to say about his work? Perhaps you could tell him not to
worry. I was quite pleasantly surprised. He's at his best
when reporting events factually and clearly. Some of these
events that he's described have not, to my knowledge, been
written about before. They seem very personal, there's a lot
of good detail. The only motivation for a writer should be to
write the truth as he sees it. Some of the descriptions of
engagements are very moving. Yes. Very good indeed. But
the philosophy's a different matter. It's rather like poor
Tolstoy with a Marxist flavour, sort of stirred in. I had to
skip a lot of it, even at the twelfth reading. But tell him, if
you see him, never be afraid to show anyone your work. It's
the only way to learn. Some of it's sentimental, of course. I
tend to distrust sentimentality. (*Pause.*) I wonder if he read
my poems? Why do you think he never came back? Is it
because he was taken off my case? . . . can't they send
someone who can *talk* . . . or something to *read*?
(*Lights fade. The* CHEKA *man remains impassive.* GORKY's
apartment, night. MARINA *takes the thermometer away from*
GORKY.)
MARINA: Still up. Blok's widow rang, about arrangements for the
funeral. She said she knows you did your best. The permit to
leave came through.

GORKY: Did my best. Important to save lives.
MARINA: Mandelstam rang again. About Gumilyov.
>   (GORKY *throws back his head, rolls his eyes.*)
>   He said it was a matter of life and death.
GORKY: Number of times I've heard that.
MARINA: When you saw Lenin, did you . . . (*Pause.*) He said
>   the only chance now was if you could phone Lenin.
GORKY: Why don't you find yourself a younger man? I'm not
>   going to get married again.
MARINA: Really, I owe you everything. I'll stick with you. I'm
>   addicted to old reprobates.
GORKY: Good. Start making arrangements for both of us
>   tomorrow. As quickly and as secretly as possible. I'm going
>   to Capri to get better.
>   (MARINA *breathes deeply. Stands up.*)
MARINA: If only you'd seen the files I've been sending to the
>   Cheka.
GORKY: (*Sharply*) What?
MARINA: Lies, all lies.
>   (GORKY *chuckles.*)
>   Shall I try and get through to Lenin?
GORKY: (*Wearily*) It's impossible at this time of night.
MARINA: If I reach him, I'll put him through up here.
>   (*She kisses him, goes.* GORKY *very carefully disconnects the
>   phone by the bed. When he sits down, he starts to cough very
>   violently. Looks at his handkerchief.*)

(*Scene changes to: firing squad. Four* CHEKA *men lead Gumilyov
downstage and shoot him. They drag the body off.*
>   MANDELSTAM *appears as they do this.*)

MANDELSTAM: I've forgotten what I wanted to say.
>   The blind swallow on her clipped wings
>   Flies back to her temple of shadows.
>   Translucently the night delirium sings.

Grasshoppers babble. The word drowns.
On a dried-up river drifts an empty boat.
My dead swallow plummets down
With a green twig twitching in its throat.

Bring back to me the swelling joy of recognition.
Return to me my shy clairvoyant hands,
I only hear the voices of the past,
Night of forgetting, shifting sands.

Sound can fountain through the fingers
Of those with power to love and see.
But I've forgotten what I wanted to say
And the word without flesh flies back to me.

(*The Stray Dog. Wrecked.*)

AKHMATOVA: We were too late. About two days too late as it
happened. (*A silence.* MANDELSTAM *wakes* NADEZHDA.)
How can you find words to express a moan? (*She makes a
low keening noise.*) I'd like to be able to create a sound . . .
using words and meanings so that the only thing left ringing
in the ear would be . . . (*She makes the sound again. A
silence. She speaks calmly.*) I had this absurd idea today that
I'd come here and read, like the old days. I wrote Kolia a
poem because I knew inside that he was already dead. I
would come here and read it when the Club was full.
(MAYAKOVSKY *comes in, drunk, exhausted.* AKHMATOVA *and*
NADEZHDA *go.*)

MAYAKOVSKY: You go into meetings and see people sitting
there in *halves*. What's happened to them? Slaughtered?
Murdered? 'What's going on!?' you shout. It's all right . . .
they're in two meetings at the same time. 'We have to go to
twenty meetings a day so we have to split ourselves in two.'
I long for one more meeting, just one more grand meeting
to . . . discuss the abolition of all meetings!

LILI: I'm going to Berlin tomorrow for a few months. I'll write
to you.

MAYAKOVSKY: As the saying goes, the incident's closed. Love's
boat has crashed on philistine reefs.

(MAYAKOVSKY *turns his back on her. She goes.*)
Came back to sign. Guilt. Very bourgeois . . . but real
enough.

MANDELSTAM: Too late. He was shot two days ago. It wouldn't
have made any difference.

(MAYAKOVSKY *sits head in hands.*)

MAYAKOVSKY: I was jailed twice when I was fourteen. Chewed
a notebook, swallowed it. With addresses, binding. The
examining magistrate made me take dictation; charge was:
'Writing a proclamation!' I used to write 'Sokiul democritic'
as if I couldn't spell. It fooled them. Guilty but under age.
As ever. I have intervened, I have taken sides and if it tears
me apart, I am not going to change trains now. We've
discovered a common enemy, Osip, but it is not the
Revolution. I'll simply have to shout louder, that's all.

MANDELSTAM: We are all fellow travellers. (*Pause.*) In the desert.
(*He goes to the palm tree and takes down his umbrella.* TUMIN
comes in. Desolate.)

TUMIN: Do you remember that woman before the Revolution?
She filled the whole room with flowers and danced on a
looking glass with a small child dressed as Cupid? Do you
remember?

KUFTIK: No, I don't remember.
(KUFTIK *goes, swinging his cane.* MANDELSTAM *and*
MAYAKOVSKY *embrace.* TUMIN *runs out, after* KUFTIK.)

TUMIN: It was here! In this room!

MANDELSTAM: They've given us some real power now, Volodya.
(MANDELSTAM *goes, leaving* MAYAKOVSKY *in a spot.*)
(*The light fades on* MAYAKOVSKY. *But the music comes up
more jauntily. Not a dying fall.*)

Akhmatova's room.

*The door bell is ringing and ringing. A man in his twenties stands
to the side of the room.*

A woman in her sixties comes through the room: NADEZHDA

NADEZHDA: Yes? Who is it?

BOOMSTRA: I've come about the interview. I telephoned last
week. Is that Anna Akhmatova?

NADEZHDA: Who are you? What do you want?

BOOMSTRA: Boomstra. Television. From Holland.

NADEZHDA: You speak very good Russian.

BOOMSTRA: Thank you. Can I come in? We made an appointment.

(AKHMATOVA *appears*.)

NADEZHDA: It's for you. Netherlands.

AKHMATOVA: Don't be stupid. Let him in.

NADEZHDA: Am I your servant now?

(*She lets him in.*)

AKHMATOVA: Come in. Bring him in.

(BOOMSTRA *stands stiffly, fiddling with his tape recorder.*)

BOOMSTRA: Rudy Boomstra. I'm sorry, I expected to find you alone.

NADEZHDA: Do you want me to leave you alone?

AKHMATOVA: I'm too old to need a chaperone. (*Quickly to* NADEZHDA.) I've forgotten what it is he's come about.

BOOMSTRA: I've come about the interview.

AKHMATOVA: Yes. You're late.

NADEZHDA: (*To* AKHMATOVA) It doesn't bother me whether I go or stay.

BOOMSTRA: I was hoping that we could have a preliminary talk and then I can go back and see the others and work out what we're going to do.

AKHMATOVA: Who are the others?

BOOMSTRA: Just a cameraman and a sound technician.

AKHMATOVA: Oh no. That wasn't what I was expecting at all.

BOOMSTRA: I explained on the telephone.

AKHMATOVA: (*To* NADEZHDA) I've changed my mind. (*To* BOOMSTRA) A tape-recorded interview only.

BOOMSTRA: You don't understand. I work for Dutch television. Dutch television is very sympathetic. We're not here officially.

NADEZHDA: Neither are we. (*Brief glance of collusion.*) Annichka isn't used to meeting foreigners. The last one was an Englishman in 1946. Unfortunately, being vain and too old to know better, she rather fell for him and stayed all night talking and so her work was banned for another twenty years.

AKHMATOVA: Don't be silly. It wasn't his fault. He was an admirer of my work and thought I was dead.

BOOMSTRA: (*Confused*) Look, I'm so sorry. I didn't realize. I'll go right away.

AKHMATOVA: No, no. I am fully and fairly *rehabilitated*. They're letting me go to Oxford. I'm getting a degree.

NADEZHDA: Getting a degree of rope with which to hang yourself.

AKHMATOVA: Do you know anything about Russian poetry?

BOOMSTRA: Well, a little . . .

AKHMATOVA: Nadia dear, why don't you go and make some tea for us all? The young man's come to interview me. He'll get round to you when he's got a year or so to spare.
(NADEZHDA *hovers*.)

BOOMSTRA: If there isn't any danger of you being victimized . . . why not a camera?

NADEZHDA: Vanity.

AKHMATOVA: Oh do go and make some tea . . . you look completely parched dear boy.
(NADEZHDA *goes impassively*.)
Now. Let's stop messing around.

BOOMSTRA: I didn't realize you were going to have company. Is she a relative?

AKHMATOVA: Mandelstam's wife.

BOOMSTRA: Mandelstam. . . ?
(BOOMSTRA *is silent, in deep waters*.)

AKHMATOVA: The reason why I asked her to leave the room was because I want to persuade you to interview her. Instead of me.
(BOOMSTRA *is embarrassed. A pause. Switches on tape*.)

BOOMSTRA: The first thing I wanted to ask you was – Did you ever want to leave Russia?

AKHMATOVA: Never.

BOOMSTRA: Do you think suffering enriched your work?

AKHMATOVA: That's a comfortable equation. It could only come from the West. It isn't something we like to contemplate . . . I'm sorry, that was rather stern.

BOOMSTRA: No, no. That's all right. I asked for it.

AKHMATOVA: You know Stalin never said a single memorable thing in the whole of his miserable life. He managed to eat a lot of words, words that came from other people's mouths. They tried very hard to extinguish us and grind words into paste. But poetry is very odd stuff. It looks so frail but actually it's harder than a diamond. Do you understand what I mean? It's indestructible. Stalin swatted Mandelstam like a wasp. But they knew it was going to happen, he and Nadia. They knew that someone would arrive one day and take everything away in boxes. So she simply set out to memorize all his poems one by one. And she kept herself alive travelling from one end of the Soviet Union to the other until it was safe to put them on paper again. Do you understand what I'm saying to you?

BOOMSTRA: Yes. Yes, I do.

(NADEZHDA *comes back with the tea*.)

NADEZHDA: Making the tea is one thing, cleaning up all your shit is quite another matter.

BOOMSTRA: Can I ask you about your husband?

NADEZHDA: Osip . . . and I? (*A pause.*) We were two people. (*A pause.*) We fought all the time. We squabbled like cats. We made love in the night. What is there to say?

(BOOMSTRA *embarrassed*. NADEZHDA *sits*.)

Were you talking about the old days? Did I hear that? (*Chuckles.*) Do you know who I saw the other day? Tumin. Didn't he used to hang about the clubs? Yes, I know he did. He dribbles.

AKHMATOVA: Oh yes, I've seen him. Senile marasmus.

NADEZHDA: That's it. That's what he's got.

(*They both chuckle.*)

Are you going to pour the tea? Or shall I?

AKHMATOVA: I will read to you.

(*She stands up.*)

All is bartered, betrayed and bereaved
The black wing of death quivered near
All is torn by a terrible grieving
So how can this radiance appear?

(*The lights come on.* AKHMATOVA *throws off her age, to be the*

86

AKHMATOVA *of the play, alone in the spotlight as the light*
fades on the other two.)
By day a strong fragrance of cherry
Drifts from magical woods near the town
And in depths of a clear summer night
A million new galaxies drown.

Such marvels approach ever nearer
To the crumbling houses of lime
Such mysteries, shy and unfathomed
But sought out from the dawning of time.

COMMITMENTS

THE CHARACTERS

HUGH GRIFFIN
WILLIE MILNE
CLAIRE RANDALL
BUFFO COLE
INGY LUTZ
ARNIE MOSS

SCENE:

The action takes place at Hugh's flat in Earl's Court during 1973 and 1974.

ACT I: Scene 1: November 1972
        Scene 2: 28 February 1973
        Scene 3: 13 December 1973
ACT II: Scene 4: 8 January 1974
        Scene 5: 1 March 1974, 12.30 a.m.
        Scene 6: Same night, 2.00 a.m.

Commitments was first performed at the Bush Theatre, London, on 23 June 1980. The cast was as follows:

HUGH	Alan Rickman
WILL	George Irving
CLAIRE	Paola Dionisotti
INGI	Deborah Findlay
ARNIE	Jack Chissick
BUFFO	Bryan Coleman
Director	Richard Wilson
Décor	Sue Plummer

ACT I

SCENE I

In pre-set, Joni Mitchell, 'Blue'.
'. . . Acid, booze and ass,
Needles, guns and grass,
Lots of laughs, lots of laughs . . .'
Slowly fade to black.
Crossfade sound. An old man's voice, British, very deliberate,
from the stereo tuner which glows in the dark.

RADIO: I heard a good story once about one of those meetings.
It took place at Saratov, down on the Volga. It was held in a
great hall. And, at the hour fixed for it to begin, the
chairman addressed the packed audience – filling every
chair on the floor and all the standing room at the back and
sides. 'Comrades', he said – tovarishi was already in
fashion . . .

(In black crossfade from house speakers to tuner on set. Lights
slowly up on Hugh's flat; the living room. An old, elegant, none
too tidy, Earl's Court flat. Two large windows overlook the
street. Double doors to small bedroom off upstage right. The
style is accidental, but there; *accumulated and careless. An*
inherited flat – with a mixture of pre-war and modern furniture;
a Chesterfield in need of stuffing, with patterned blankets
thrown over it. A large round table, once used for dining, is now
mostly piled with books, magazines and papers. A Habitat
sofa, a 'director's chair and four Victorian wooden chairs. A
Victorian fringed shade on a standard lamp, and a thirties one.
A couple of other lamps; an anglepoise. On the floor, worn rugs
over varnished floor. Upstage centre double doors to rest of flat.
Cream walls and paintwork, not new. The room is dominated
by books, from waist level to ceiling. Stage right of the hall door
there is a large noticeboard, six feet square, covered with bills,
notes, press cuttings, instamatic prints, birthday cards,
mementoes. There are some bottles of drink and glasses in various
places. A telephone on a long lead. A shelf of magazines; Oz,
Time Out, *old copies of* Seven Days, Black Dwarf. *A piano.*)

RADIO: . . . 'Comrades, there are hundreds of comrades here who want to get in. Will those of you who have seats, please move forward as far as you can.' Then there was a great scraping of chairs as everybody dragged his chair a few inches forward, and room was made for a few hundred more eager listeners at the back. The chairman stepped forward again . . .

HUGH: (*Voice off*) Hang on . . .

(*The hall doors are pulled open, but for the moment no one comes through them.*)

CLAIRE: (*Voice off*) Will it go. . . ?

HUGH: (*Voice off*) Right, then. One, two, three . . .

RADIO: . . . 'Comrades, there are still comrades outside, and many of them have never yet been able to attend a meeting. Will those of you who have already had a meeting please go out and give a chance to those comrades who have been less lucky.' And some hundreds of people got up . . .

CLAIRE: (*Off*) Shit.

RADIO: . . . and walked out, leaving their seats for their unfortunate brethren who had never had the treat of being present at a political meeting.

(*Large object blocks the doorway.* HUGH's *and* CLAIRE's *faces can be seen now.*)

HUGH: God almighty.

CLAIRE: Won't it go?

HUGH: He may have to lose his steering arm.

RADIO: That's what the Revolution meant in its early stages – a grand, universal blowing off of long suppressed political steam.

(*The object is manoeuvred through the doorway and into the room. Huge, papier-mâché cartoon model of Edward Heath, in sailor's garb.* CLAIRE *and* HUGH *stand exhausted.*)

HUGH: Over there, I think.

RADIO: I was reminded of Wordsworth's lines about the French Revolution . . .

CLAIRE: I told you we'd got a lot of junk.

RADIO: 'Bliss was it then to be alive, but to be young was very heaven.'

(*Blackout.*)

Radio light glows in dark. Sound continues. A Russian voice, thick with age and self-pity, almost indecipherable.

RADIO: So far I have hunger, I have cold, I have no clothes. And not me alone because all the people was suffering the same way. I was witnessed, on the street, falling people from hunger. They don't have what to eat for weeks. They fall like flies. So, I don't think so this people was happy about it, all thing what going on. Well, what I gonna tell you?

(Crossfade into Lavrov's version of the 'Marseillaise' – 'The Workers' Marseillaise' sung by a Russian choir.

Lights slowly up.

The room is as before, but the Heath model is in the corner, half covered up.

There is daylight through the closed blinds, but two lamps and an anglepoise are still on.

HUGH *is asleep or dozing at the round table; his bloody hand on pile of colour supplements.*

WILL *in. In bathrobe, carrying book, bowl of cereal. Goes to window, half opens blinds. They are both in their twenties.*

HUGH *is middle class, fashionable, but very casually dressed.*

WILL *is working class; a Geordie actor. Good-looking, solid and not stupid.* HUGH *groans.)*

WILL: Morning, Nicolai Nicolievich.

HUGH: *(Throaty)* Vasily Vasilievich.

WILL: A hard night digging up the tundra?

HUGH: A hard night indeed, Vasily Vasilievich. But today I am to be promoted.

WILL: Congratulations.

HUGH: They are giving me a spade. Is the samovar on?

WILL: Boiling, tovarish.

(WILL *over to stereogram. The song continues triumphantly.)*

HUGH: The words mean 'We renounce the old world, we shake its dust off our feet.'

WILL: Where's whatsername?

(HUGH *rotates finger and stabs it towards the door.*)
She'll be back for her sewing machine.

HUGH: Reckon that's all right, then?

WILL: Yeah.

(HUGH *lifts up hand. Paper comes up with it.* WILL *consults the book,* Das Kapital.)

WILL: What's it mean by *discontinuous* nature of reproduction?

HUGH: Oh look, I've bled all over the funeral suit of Princess Wan Tan of the Western Han dynasty.

WILL: The three forms of capital. The nature of reproduction is *discontinuous.*

(WILL *over to the table, sits down.*)

HUGH: Give us a break.

WILL: Your girlfriend must have taken exception to the liver.

HUGH: We had liver?

WILL: You tucked it in your flies. Raw. It was a joke. I think.

(*Starts to eat his cornflakes.*)

HUGH: Oh, God.

WILL: She must have thought you were trying to tell her something.

(*Pause. Eats.*)

You beat up the kitchen a bit. I've cleared it up, mostly.

HUGH: I was trying to tell her something. She kept quoting Tom Wolfe. I can't stand him. I read one of his books, reluctantly. *The Redcurrant-Flavoured, Macho-Mint Pool Queen*, or something like that. Like having an enema with Seven-Up.

(WILL *opens* Das Kapital.)

HUGH: Volume Two already?

WILL: Didn't have One in the library. It makes me feel so *dense*.

HUGH: Right, there're three forms of Capital. Money Capital. Production Capital. Commodity Capital. It's evolutionary. Right? Frogspawn, tadpole, frog. Object being to produce more and more frogspawn. And so on.

WILL: Yeah, I've just about grasped that.

HUGH: Yeah, but they're all swimming around in the pond at the same time. Out of synch. The turnover cycle produces a lot of frogs but they don't all snuff it before the next cycle begins. It's discontinuous.

WILL: Right. So where does the use-value of the commodity come in?

(HUGH *does mock collapse, very quick. Takes the book. Passes his hand over his eyes.*)

HUGH: 'The formula for the circuit of money capital is M dash C dot dot dot P dot dot dot C stroke dash M stroke. The dots indicate that the circulation process is interrupted, while C stroke and M stroke denote an increase in C and M as a result of surplus value.'

WILL: Were you up all night?

(HUGH *nods.*)

I gave you two Mogadon. I thought they might calm you down. They didn't seem to work. I felt like sueing Roche's.

HUGH: I had some amphetamines. Present from our American friend.

(*Shows small paper packet.*)

De uppers counteract de downers. Base line and flute. Sort of a cocktail.

(WILL *stares at* HUGH.)

Don't look at me like that.

(*Pause.* WILL *finishes eating.*)

I'm *depressed*, for godsake.

WILL: I would be if I'd had that lot.

(*Takes* Daily Mail *out of dressing-gown pocket. Drops it in front of* HUGH. *Gets up, goes out with cereal bowl.* HUGH *opens paper, then gets up, wanders to the door. Bit unsteady. Stands looking down hall towards kitchen.*)

HUGH: What about this then. 'Have at Ye! City insurance broker Paul Ingham-Smith seen here on the attack. Taking cover is Aslef driver George Carter, 53, (arrowed in cab). Mr Ingham-Smith's improvised bayonet, a folding umbrella with a Marlin spike cunningly attached, will get many an admiring glance from fellow commuters when the rail strike starts in earnest this morning.'

(*Grimaces, drops paper delicately on the floor.*)

(*Off*) You ought to get all three volumes of *Capital* and just read the introductions. You may think it's cheating but it still adds up to three hundred pages and they're much better written.

(WILL *in with tray, tea, biscuits, letters.*)

WILL: I didn't know you had to have a degree in maths to understand it.

(HUGH *toes the* Mail *gingerly.*)

HUGH: Did somebody give you a subscription to this?

WILL: Ah well, you see, it gives you an idea what the right wing are thinking about.

(HUGH *stares back impassively.*)

I get it for the gossip column.

(HUGH *picks up the newspaper.* WILL *pours out some tea.*)

HUGH: I'll cut this out for Claire.

WILL: She didn't come back last night.

(HUGH *goes over to the table and picks up a letter, glances at* WILL. *Opens letter, takes out cheque.*)

HUGH: I'm going to get a regular job. Eighteen quid for that piece on the Grocer. I risked my health going through his rubbish. It cost me a tenner to bribe the dustman. It was the exposé of the month.

WILL: That he uses dental floss?

HUGH: It staggered *me*.

(*Pause.*

WILL *looks up. Takes a copy of another paper from the tray.* HUGH *looks at cornflakes sickly.*)

Joke.

(*Pause.* WILL *reads.* HUGH *breaks an amphetamine capsule over his cornflakes.*)

What does a certain Trotskyist daily paper have to say this morning?

WILL: There's an economic crisis.

HUGH: No!

WILL: Good article about Chile. Says Allende's about to cock it up. Hasn't dissolved the old constitution, hasn't properly taken power.

HUGH: Snap, crackle, pop.

(*Starts to eat cornflakes.*)

What's happened to Claire?

WILL: She had two meetings last night. Pinewood. Then another in Watford. Appears to have spent the night elsewhere. No doubt for some principled reason.

HUGH: She obviously forgot about the rail strike.

WILL: Come on.

HUGH: Well . . .

WILL: You mean she goes to a meeting to talk about the rail strike and forgets there are no trains after midnight?

HUGH: It's just possible. (*Taking the paper.*) 'Comrades, this Tory government has stepped up its increasingly vicious attacks on the working class. With one snivelling stroke they have increased the price of bread by a whole half pee and made it impossible for people without credit cards to get access to Gracie Fields concerts. Make no mistake, this crisis cannot be resolved by mere wage demands for only when the working class prepare to take state power can . . . continued page ninety four . . .'

(*This is as cynically provocative as possible but in a misguided way is still an attempt to cheer. He tickles* WILL *with edge of the paper.* WILL *impassive.*)

WILL: You ought to bloody well join the League, instead of fannying around on the fringes. I mean, all these shelves are crammed with political theory. You know five times as much about Marxism as me. You know modern Russian history backwards.

HUGH: Yeah well, when I was at school I read everything there was to know about the Great War. Did I have to volunteer as a nurse?

WILL: You ought to *use* your knowledge more.

HUGH: That's a bit soggy. Where's the Marxist imperative? Aren't I supposed to join to stop fascism? Isn't capitalism going to push us into a nuclear holocaust?

WILL: You know the arguments better than I do.

HUGH: The working class aren't eating boot polish yet. Things will have to get a lot worse before I intervene to avert the World Economic Crisis.

WILL: But you fancy yourself as a Marxist.

HUGH: I don't want to join the revolutionary party, that's all.

WILL: Fine.

HUGH: As far as I'm concerned we live in a liberal democracy.

As far as you're concerned we live in a Police State. I sleep at night, you don't.

WILL: You don't sleep at all. Look at you.

HUGH: Well . . . I meant, metaphorically.

WILL: You're a political Peeping Tom.

HUGH: You'll never make a zealot, my son.

WILL: Where is that bloody woman? What time is it? Why didn't she phone?

HUGH: Not her style.

WILL: She might have got smashed up in a car.

HUGH: I think you'd have heard by now.

(WILL *gets up from the table and goes over to the telephone.*)

WILL: I'm going to phone someone in the party.

HUGH: Don't be a prick.

(WILL *dials.*)

There has to be an easier way.

(CLAIRE *comes in. Her large shoulder bag is crammed with papers and leaflets. She's a little older than the others and is disguising her glamour behind scarves and books and a loose coat.*)

CLAIRE: Don't say anything. I'm sorry.

(WILL *poised with receiver, guilty.*)

What are you doing?

(WILL *replaces the receiver.*)

WILL: I was worried. I was phoning the police.

(CLAIRE *puts the bag down. Takes out a package. Goes over to low table by the sofa. Very calm.*)

CLAIRE: You don't need to dial. Just lift up the receiver and you'll get straight through to a special branch constable in Wilton street.

(*Unwraps the package.*)

I got us a cake.

(*Heavy silence.* CLAIRE *takes off coat and scarf, goes out into the hall with them.* HUGH *looks over at* WILL, *then tactfully slips off into the bedroom.* CLAIRE *back in.*)

WILL: You must think I'm very naïve.

CLAIRE: The meeting was late. I missed the last train.

(WILL *stares through her.*)

I stayed with some comrades in Elstree. There wasn't a phone.

(WILL *looks at the floor, rubs the top of his head.*)

I slept on the floor. Badly.

WILL: How was the meeting?

CLAIRE: It looked like being a disaster. We put up a motion to occupy the studios, but the Stalinists wanted a 'work-in'. It's incredible, after the experience of Upper Clyde, which *they* see as a victory. A victory! Two thousand jobs lost, a four year no-strike agreement and a slave labour contract with an American monopoly subsidized by the Tories. If that's what the British Communist Party calls a victory, God help the working class if they ever get defeated.

WILL: And that took you all night?

CLAIRE: It wasn't the only thing on the agenda. We put up a motion calling on the union to instruct the TUC to call a general strike to bring down the Tories.

WILL: How did that go down?

CLAIRE: (*Grins*) Scared the life out of 'em. Sniggers of derision from IS and IMG who of course were cuddling up to the Stalinists like mad. Stalinists tried everything to stop us speaking, calling us out of order, trying to set a time limit, but of course the IMG, being mad about spontaneity, were reluctantly, *very* reluctantly forced to support us.

WILL: Great. So?

CLAIRE: We won. Easily. Since they couldn't exactly vote *against* a motion that proposed actually doing something about bringing down the Tories.

WILL: Except when it goes up to the Executive of the union, they'll water it down or turn it into a one day *protest* strike or something.

CLAIRE: Well, we sort the Leadership out next. Don't be so negative.

WILL: I'm just being realistic.

CLAIRE: You wouldn't know. You haven't actually been there. Despite the fact that no films are getting made, honestly there's a real feeling of optimism. And there's a real feeling of comradeship now that the railwaymen are coming out as well.

(*Pause. She pulls a face.*)
Which is more than can be said for the atmosphere here.
(*Goes across to* WILL. *Puts her hands on his shoulders.*)
I love you very much. I missed you. I spent a very
uncomfortable night.
(*Half nod from* WILL.)

WILL: You have to give Marge an answer about the tour.
Today. She rang up in a panic last night. It's tied up with
getting visas and things. Here.
(*Goes over to the round table and tears off a sheet of notepad.*
CLAIRE *collapses on a chair, tense, tired.* WILL *hands her the*
scribbled notes.)

CLAIRE: God.

WILL: It's a long one.

CLAIRE: Edinburgh, Belfast, Amsterdam, Stockholm, Bonn,
Prague . . . I can't go to Prague, can I?
(WILL *shrugs, slightly annoyed.*)
You make the decision for me.

WILL: For seven thousand pounds, I'd perform in the *Kremlin*.

CLAIRE: It's three months.
(*Stares at paper.* HUGH *back in, changed.*)
I can't go away for that long. I'll be in complete retreat
from politics by the time I get back.

WILL: We owe three months' rent.

HUGH: There's no hurry. I'm quite flush at the moment.
(WILL *makes an impotent gesture.* CLAIRE *flops back.*)

CLAIRE: I'll be shoved in as support to a second-division heavy
metal band like Black Sabbath or Vinegar Joe, whose hotel
behaviour will be akin to the massed armies of Genghis
Khan on leave. Sleep will be impossible at any hour of the
night. Room service will be occupied until the morning
putting out small fires and ejecting unwanted visitors. My
backing group will consist of some ex-*sultans of swing* from
Cheshire who have not surfaced since the trad boom and if
they've ever played together before they're not admitting it.
They'll drink too much lager, get maudlin about their
wives, call me 'love' and insult foreigners. Then when it
finally sinks in that I'm not going to fuck any of them,

they'll turn into a tight little group and drop heavy hints that I'm not professional. They'll enjoy the blues numbers and everything by Billie Holliday but play insensitively on anything that's written after 1960, and by a woman. About two days before we come home, so I won't think badly of them, they'll relent and start behaving like considerate elder brothers. After I've paid *you* the rent, given my agent her 15% and half the rest to the fighting fund, I might be able to afford a new pair of tights.

HUGH: Won't the Central Committee disapprove?

CLAIRE: (*Snaps*) I don't know. (*Pause.*) Oh, I can't do it, I know I can't.

(WILL *walks out of the room.*)

God, I don't know, what do you think?

(HUGH *is looking for something on the big table. He moves a pile of new copies of the League's daily paper. Shrugs, sympathetic.*) What happened to your hand?

HUGH: I was practising clenched fist salutes with a packet of razor blades.

CLAIRE: You're a funny colour.

HUGH: I broke a soda syphon. I was trying to get the little glass tube out.

CLAIRE: You see, the crisis is getting to you, too. You'll go mad. Your head's full of theory but you don't know what to do with it. You're frightened of joining the working class. You have to go out into the real world – sell the paper, talk at meetings, argue with workers, recruit the youth – all those things mean *practising* Communism. It's dirty, you get into conflict, but by Christ all those dry text books start to really *mean* something. Look at you! You're a mass of contradictions. Generous and kind to a fault, but totally absorbed by seedy little pleasures. Trying to carve out a literary career as a Marxist intellectual but pathologically incapable or unwilling to talk to a single member of the working class. And it's all written on your face, you look like *death*.

(HUGH *ignores* CLAIRE *for a couple of beats. Continues rummaging on the table.*)

HUGH: I've just finished translating some Soviet poets. It's quite recent. They're an improvement on Yevtushenko. Thought you might like to read . . .
(*Finds another pile of newspapers.*)
Are you trying to turn this place into a branch office?

CLAIRE: Those are the local deliveries.

HUGH: Are they? I don't know. A rather scruffy German girl brought them.

CLAIRE: They should have been done last night. That's Ingy. Was she late?

HUGH: She dropped them in around ten.

CLAIRE: Sod Will. He's so *undisciplined*. He's got this simple sentimental idea about Communism. It's just got to be knocked out of him.

HUGH: Well. I may have been a bit of a handful last night. So don't be too hard on him.

CLAIRE: I'm too bloody soft as it is.

HUGH: That isn't anything to be ashamed of.

CLAIRE: I expect it'll all fizzle out in a couple of weeks. My amours all go the same way. They don't run away from me, they run away from the party. I don't think I've got the stamina any more. He's very demanding. He eats and fucks for two people. That's very nice, of course, I'm not complaining about the sex . . . Oh God, home comforts are nice though aren't they?
(*She curls up on the sofa under a rug.*)
Now I can decide whether to have a sleep, a shower . . . Mmmmm! When Will left his wife we stayed in some terrible places. The last and most dreadful was a cameraman friend of Will's in Ealing. They were practically in the Monday Club and they took us in, knowing what our politics were. They used to wait up for us. Very friendly, of course – two in the morning, you're completely shagged out from some meeting – there would be Nick and Sue, in their night things, the hot chocolate simmering, like a couple of tarantulas. 'What are you going to do with *us* when you take over? Har, har. Send us to *Siberia*? Har, har . . . But, seriously Claire, there has to be some control over the unions.' Thank God we met you.

HUGH: It's a big flat. I don't like living on my own.

CLAIRE: I wanted to ask you another favour.

HUGH: Er, yes . . .

CLAIRE: About Ingy.

HUGH: The kraut with the dirty hair.

CLAIRE: She lives in a terrible cupboard off Redcliffe Gardens. It's nineteen quid a week, which she can't afford, because she doesn't have a grant any more and it has leopard skin wallpaper. Honestly. She's been getting very depressed . . .

HUGH: I noticed . . .

CLAIRE: So I thought . . . the junk room. You could clear out all your Arthur Ransome books and cricket bats . . .

HUGH: I think I'm getting your drift.

CLAIRE: She'd pay some rent.

HUGH: A complete *putsch* of my living space.

CLAIRE: She's much more fun than she appears. I like her very, very much. I mean, living conditions completely affect your personality . . .

HUGH: Couple of hot baths and we'll be swapping anecdotes about Günther Grass and sharing a bottle of Heineken. Is that what you mean?

CLAIRE: She's very bright. She's just finished at St Mary's. Obviously I'd like to have another woman here. Make a change from the locker room chat.

HUGH: All right. I don't mind.

CLAIRE: You look as if you're going to puke.

HUGH: I embrace my destiny.

(WILL *comes in, very tense.*)

CLAIRE: I'm going to have a shower. Are you sure you're all right? You look bloody strange to me.

(*Notices* WILL.)

You're making a terrible atmosphere. Go away.

WILL: How do you think *I* feel? I haven't worked for six months.

CLAIRE: Just leave me ten minutes to myself.

WILL: Seven thousand pounds is two years' wages to me.

(CLAIRE *goes out through hall.* WILL *breathing heavily, bull-like.* HUGH *starts to get stomach cramps. Rocks gently backwards and forwards.*)

You've been a good friend to me.

(HUGH *grimaces*.)

Can I ask you a *personal* question?

HUGH: Fire away.

WILL: Do you think I'm any good?

HUGH: Er . . .

WILL: Well, that answers my question.

HUGH: No. I was thinking. You've got a lot of energy.

WILL: But no technique . . . *uncontrolled* energy.

HUGH: Well . . . I think the amount of energy you put in . . .
often solves your technical problems.

(HUGH *palms a pill, quickly*.)

WILL: What the hell are you taking now?

HUGH: Rennies.

WILL: But not always.

HUGH: Sorry? No, not always. But, then . . .

WILL: Have you seen me be very bad?

HUGH: No. Definitely not.

WILL: Have you seen me do anything else but, you know . . . to
type?

HUGH: No . . .

(HUGH *doubles up again, smiles through it*.)

WILL: Anything without a northern accent?

HUGH: No . . .

WILL: I sound as if I've got my balls caught in a gin trap.

HUGH: You could try voice classes.

WILL: Thanks a million.

HUGH: No, I mean . . . all problems are soluble.

WILL: I can't spend the rest of my life doing beer commercials
and playing simple Geordie fishermen. Politics is the only
thing that's ever given me any self-respect. I'm like a
bulldog with a bone, I know, I can't leave it alone. But if I
don't get a job soon, she won't carry on fancying me, will
she?

HUGH: But . . . you give the appearance of enormous
self-confidence.

WILL: Ah well, I'll work on the vulnerability more.

HUGH: I'm sorry, I meant . . .

WILL: She needs me. She needs someone to look after her. She's hopeless. I feel so . . .
(*Lets out a roar of frustration.*)
I dunno. I reckon I'm an improvement on the others. She used to live with this dreadful xylophone player.
HUGH: I heard.
WILL: He was an aggressive xylophone player. Beat her up.
HUGH: Bad vibes.
(WILL *gives* HUGH *an old-fashioned look.*)
WILL: Then I had to pick up the pieces after that media shit had pissed off back to his wife and kids.
HUGH: Roy Johnson.
WILL: You'd think people in a left wing party would behave different.
HUGH: She doesn't mention him much.
WILL: He did a big number on her. She was his political protégée. She's been on valium ever since.
HUGH: The best of us have no control over our lives. Blame the economic crisis. It's easy.
(CLAIRE *in, in dressing-gown, carrying towel. Followed by* BUFFO. *About sixty, slightly military. Not camp. Dark blue overcoat, quite smartly dressed.*)
CLAIRE: Hugh . . .
(CLAIRE *ducks out again.* HUGH *doubles up again.*)
HUGH: Buffo.
BUFFO: Need a bit of advice. You all right?
HUGH: Just eaten something I shouldn't have.
BUFFO: Tod's not too bright today. I've got him tucked up in bed with Lytton Strachey.
HUGH: Lucky Tod.
BUFFO: It's just a bit of liver trouble.
HUGH: Sorry to hear it.
BUFFO: He's bloody poor company. I can tell you that.
WILL: We all are at the moment.
BUFFO: Saw you on the box last night.
WILL: Yeah?
BUFFO: Least I think it was you. The advertisement. 'It's what your right arm's for.'

WILL: Oh, aye . . .

(WILL *smiles wanly and looks down at the floor.*)

HUGH: How's Mr Volvo, Buff? Keeping you busy?

BUFFO: Can't complain. Bringing out a new model soon. Three layers of armour plating with an electric blanket between each one. Gas-fired central heating. Christmas decorations optional. Not that this humble clerk could ever afford one.

(CLAIRE *back in.* WILL *gets up and leaves.* HUGH *has grabbed the paper again.* CLAIRE *pours* BUFFO *a neat gin, glancing after* WILL.)

CLAIRE: (*At* WILL) Child.

(*Takes drink over to* BUFFO.)

Commuter's breakfast.

BUFFO: I didn't come for this. But thanks.

(HUGH *tries to focus on the paper.*)

HUGH: Keep still!

BUFFO: Had a little legal enquiry.

HUGH: Burgess and Maclean, Burgess and Maclean . . .

BUFFO: Wondered if any of you *intelligent* folks could help.

(*Drinks.*)

Cheers.

CLAIRE: I don't know if any of us know anything about the law, Buffo.

BUFFO: What was that, Hugh?

HUGH: Burgess and Maclean. More startling revelations.

BUFFO: Owes me a hundred pounds.

HUGH: Who does?

BUFFO: Guy Burgess. Just cleared off. It was a lot of money in those days.

HUGH: You can't trust these Communists.

CLAIRE: Have a seat, Buffo.

(*She motions him into a chair.*)

BUFFO: Probably spent it corrupting some young tart from Chelsea barracks. I can't stay long.

(*He sits. Muffled farting noise. Looks under the cushion, pulls out small rubber bag. Reads the writing.*)

'Emits a loud . . .' So that's what a Bronx cheer is.

(CLAIRE, *straight-faced, holds out her hand for it. Takes it, puts it in her dressing-gown.*)

HUGH: Somebody once accused her of not having a sense of humour. These bad practical jokes are the tragic result.

CLAIRE: Well, come on Buffo, out with it.

HUGH: You want advice on how to get the money back?

BUFFO: No. Story as follows. Young Tod is the sitting tenant down below. Has been since the war. Lease all legal etcetera, rent controlled. I'm just a gentleman who turned up for a visit fifteen years ago and stayed on.

HUGH: Sounds about right.

BUFFO: Indeed. Cheers. Kiss John Wolfenden's arse. It's a pretty good deal. Twelve pounds a month isn't making the landlord's fortune. He could probably sell a ninety-nine year lease for fifteen thousand if he could get rid of us, but he can't. I won't pretend the low rent hasn't been handy for us. Tod's career hasn't exactly flourished. As an interior designer he's rather trad – gold leaf, brocade; that sort of thing. And I shall be looking for my gold watch soon. Problem is, what's my legal status if Tod pops off before me? I know he's only fifty, he's a kid, but . . . I've started to worry about these things. They could chuck me out, couldn't they? Off to the YMCA and too young to be kissed.

CLAIRE: Surely, you've got a solicitor, Buffo?

BUFFO: Bwooh, shudder! Never touch 'em. Far too pricey. Charge you a grand for addressing a postcard. My cousin's got one. But . . . I don't want to involve family. Obvious reasons.

HUGH: Get married.

BUFFO: Quite, but in case Caxton Hall cuts up a bit rough . . . any other suggestions?

HUGH: Probably find out for you, Buff.

BUFFO: Would you be so kind, Hugh? Would you?

HUGH: No problem. I know a brief or two.

BUFFO: I'm so grateful. (*Drains gin, stands.*) Oh, and . . . I know I'm an old cadger but, could I borrow a roll of lavvy paper? We're a bit in need and the bloody supermarket's

shut for Ramadan or something. (*All gesture, yes.*) There
was something else I meant to return to you. What was it?
It'll come to me later. Anyway, I must love you, and leave
you. A million bills of lading await.

(*Turns at the door, to* CLAIRE. *Blows a raspberry. Goes.*)

CLAIRE: I can't think about the life they lead. It makes me
depressed.

(HUGH *goes over to the phone.*)

They haven't *been* anywhere for months.

HUGH: You do see the occasional Fortnum and Mason van
arriving.

CLAIRE: You know that phone's tapped, don't you?

HUGH: Rubbish.

(HUGH *dials.*)

And the unmistakeable smell of rancid grouse in the
autumn. They do all right.

CLAIRE: If they took out six hundred warrants last year, you can
assume they didn't bother in a thousand more cases.

HUGH: I'm not exactly a threat to the capitalist system. (*Into
phone.*) Bernard?

CLAIRE: No, but *I* am.

HUGH: OK, I'll hold.

CLAIRE: Why don't you come to another meeting at Roy's?
You'll be amazed who turns up. All kinds of people are
getting involved.

HUGH: They've been having those meetings since '68.
Everybody exhausts themselves arguing and then about ten
o'clock Jimmy Mulroy, or somebody else from the Central
Committee, turns up and delivers a twenty-minute lecture
on dialectical materialism. Everybody is so impressed by his
bull-like charisma that nobody dare argue with him.
Everybody feels uncomfortable and drifts off home.

CLAIRE: It just isn't like that any more. There's a completely
different atmosphere.

HUGH: I can't understand the dogged logic of recruiting youth,
and workers and intellectuals on completely separate fronts.
It's so calculating.

CLAIRE: But it works. That's all you should worry about.

(INGY *comes in, followed by* WILL. *Stands uncertainly.* WILL *stays by the door.*)

HUGH: (*Belfast*) Brendan, is that yeoy? I've got the rocket launchers.

CLAIRE: Hello Ingy. (*To* HUGH.) That's not funny.

WILL: (*To* CLAIRE) I'm sorry.

CLAIRE: What are you sorry about?

WILL: Can we go somewhere else?

HUGH: (*Belfast*) Escort van. Outside the National Liberal Club. Registration C for Charlie . . . Bernie! Hugh. Hello.

CLAIRE: I *still* haven't had a shower!

INGY: I left my bag here, that's all.

WILL: (*To* CLAIRE) Whose sleeping bag were *you* in last night? (INGY *takes a wooden chair by the door, watches the scene impassively.*)

HUGH: Is it true you don't charge for telephone advice? (*Pause.*) I see. Fine. Byee! (*To* CLAIRE.) He does. (*Replaces the receiver, dials again.*)

CLAIRE: (*To* WILL) Do we have to go through all that again? That was last year.

WILL: Another *sleeping bag* job, was it?

HUGH: This is Hugh Griffin, can I speak . . . OK fine, I'll hold.

CLAIRE: You're pathetic . . .

WILL: What was his name? Clive Roberts? What an asset to World Socialism *he* turned out to be.

CLAIRE: (*To* INGY) We were doing a political cabaret in Jarrow, at the Labour Club. We had to sleep on the floor. Most of us were exhausted and turned in. But he and some others went off on a tour of the clubs . . .

WILL: Yeah, and what did I find when I got back. . . ?

CLAIRE: I was explaining . . .

WILL: You were hell . . .

CLAIRE: Listen, we were reading . . .

WILL: In the same sleeping bag as . . .

CLAIRE: It was freezing.

WILL: Going at it like two ferrets in a sock.

CLAIRE: I was trying to explain the transitional programme.

WILL: You were fucking.

CLAIRE: You were drunk.

WILL: You were fucking.

CLAIRE: Leave me alone!

(CLAIRE *goes out through hall doors, past* WILL, *who tries to stop her. She brushes him off. He goes out after her.*)

HUGH: OK . . . fine . . . no, I'll ring back.

(*Replaces receiver.*)

INGY: Did you see my bag?

HUGH: What's it look like?

INGY: It's kind of old, leather.

HUGH: This place is full of bags. Some days it looks like Gucci's after a bomb attack.

INGY: It isn't valuable or anything. It's a . . . er Gladstone. Belonged to my father.

(CLAIRE *comes back in.* INGY *about to speak.*)

CLAIRE: I don't want to talk . . . sorry . . .

INGY: (*To* HUGH) It's sentimental value only . . . but . . .

(WILL *comes back in.* CLAIRE *goes to bedroom door.*)

CLAIRE: Stop following me. Is there nowhere in this place I can be on my own?

WILL: Listen . . .

(CLAIRE *into bedroom.*)

CLAIRE: Go away!

INGY: When are you going to join us then, Hugh?

(*Sound of door being locked.*)

WILL: Listen, Claire . . .

CLAIRE: It's locked now. So go away!

HUGH: (*To* INGY) Listen, I've had a bad day so far . . .

INGY: Yes, and the stock market, too.

HUGH: I've sold all my shares.

INGY: Yes, everybody is buying gold. Capitalism is floating on this sea of worthless paper money. Doesn't this worry you?

HUGH: No.

INGY: It's worth more than a hundred dollars an ounce.

(WILL *draws a chair up against the door. Speaks softly.*)

WILL: Can't . . . can't we talk about this amicably?

INGY: What are you going to do about it?

CLAIRE: Go away!

HUGH: Sell my cufflinks?

WILL: I never *see* you.

CLAIRE: (*Very loud, off*) Try coming to a few more meetings!

INGY: Have you read this Brigadier Kitson, and his low
intensity operations? And what's his name, Clutterbuck?
They're preparing people for a military takeover if things
get rough. Do you think this military exercise at Heathrow
was for the sake of a few terrorists? What were they doing,
running around in blocks of flats up there? (INGY *notices
cake.*)

WILL: Please, Claire . . .

CLAIRE: Go away!

INGY: Can I have some of that?

(CLAIRE *can be heard crying behind the door.* HUGH *gestures,*
INGY *takes some cake.*)

WILL: Don't cry, pet.

INGY: It's precisely to prepare people to accept the presence of
British soldiers on the streets, hand in glove with the police,
like in Belfast. But this time they won't be using troops
against the IRA but against the working class, against *trade
unionists*. This is good.

(INGY *tucks in.* HUGH *goes to pour* WILL *a Scotch.* WILL *is
looking down at the floor, head in hands.* CLAIRE *still crying.*
HUGH *over to* WILL *with drink.* WILL *brushes it aside.* INGY
is eating ravenously.)

HUGH: When did you eat last?

INGY: Breakfast. Yesterday.

WILL: (*Still to the door*) I don't mean to cause you pain, pet.

INGY: It's OK I'm used to it. There wasn't much food around
when I was born. '46, you know . . .

(HUGH *affected by this.* INGY *carries on eating.*)

WILL: I can't talk to you through a door!

INGY: This Tory government can't survive without the most
vicious attacks on the standard of living of the working
class.

WILL: Can't we go and eat somewhere? I can't talk to you
through a door.

HUGH: Well, you know, people have survived worse . . .

INGY: So what about the Industrial Relations Act? Legal right to picket. Wham! Gone! After centuries of struggle. This was what the pageant was about. We put on this enormous play which showed how these rights were won in England; at Jarrow and Peterloo and in the Taff Vale. And we had workers from the areas performing alongside actors. This showed me the strength of our movement . . .

HUGH: Yes . . .

INGY: We hired the Empire Pool There were ten thousand there.

HUGH: I was there.

INGY: Then you saw.

WILL: I can't talk to you through a door!
(*Silence.* CLAIRE *crying quietly.* HUGH *getting uncomfortable in the atmosphere.*)

HUGH: I think, maybe . . .

INGY: This is on the agenda. Right?
(CLAIRE *still crying.*)
You are a capitalist state. Right?

HUGH: Right.

INGY: Your monetary system is ruined. Your markets collapse. You have to go to war. Lenin knew this. He said this in 1914. Capitalism inevitably leads to war.

HUGH: But it's also responsible for peace. In between the wars.

INGY: Ah yes, the old bourgeois historian's lie. Perpetrated by A. G. P. Taylor and his cronies.

WILL: CLAIRE!
(WILL *begins to cry.*)

HUGH: A.J.P. Look, Ingy . . .
(HUGH *stands up, embarrassed* . . .)

INGY: So this is why we have a daily paper. To explain to workers what is really going on in the world. That the capitalist system will lead to chaos and barbarism.

HUGH: Well, yes . . .

INGY: It's the truth.

HUGH: What is truth . . . I don't know.

WILL: I wasn't saying it to hurt you.

INGY: But you recognize the need to get the Tories out.

HUGH: Ye . . . es . . .

CLAIRE: Liar!

WILL: No!

INGY: If you can support our polices, you can sell the paper.

WILL: No!

CLAIRE: Lies, lies, lies, lies, lies, lies.

INGY: (*Following* HUGH *to the door*) You could do a BBC sale or something. You'll meet some people you know there.

HUGH: That's what I'm worried about.

INGY: It's always a struggle. It's not like a religion. Some kind of instant enlightenment.

(HUGH *has gone, gesturing her to hold on and registering agreement at the same time.*)

WILL: All right, I'm a liar. If that's what you want. I'm a liar. (*Silence.* WILL *pulls himself together, gets up.* INGY *stares at him. He looks blankly back.*)

INGY: I left this leather bag here. Yesterday.

WILL: Yes . . .

INGY: Like a *Gladstone*.

WILL: I don't know . . .

INGY: It's very important to find this.

WILL: Under the sofa. . . ?

INGY: It was my father's. He was a non-conformist preacher. (INGY *dives behind the sofa. Lifts it from the back.*)

WILL: I'm going away.

INGY: It's not there.

WILL: I'm going to *emigrate*.

INGY: You can't. You have to do the branch deliveries this week. Sure, it's a very good solution. There could be a General Strike any time. People's bottles are going all over the place. Don't think I don't know this. Don't think this doesn't frighten me.

WILL: Have you ever heard the word 'sensitivity'? (INGY *bursts into tears.* WILL *looks shocked and puts an arm round her.*)

WILL: I'm sorry. You just . . .

INGY: It's not that. If I lose this bag, I'm just going to die. (*Sobs quietly.* CLAIRE *comes quietly out of the bedroom.*)

I know I brought it here.

CLAIRE: You sod. Leave her alone.

WILL: Jesus Christ!

(WILL *rushes out.* CLAIRE *goes over to* INGY, *puts an arm round her.*)

CLAIRE: Listen. Hugh says it's all right if you move in here. You're obviously getting depressed.

INGY: He didn't say anything.

CLAIRE: You can have the spare room.

INGY: I really need to find my bag.

CLAIRE: We'll find it.

INGY: I'm not sleeping too good.

CLAIRE: It's probably the wallpaper. I think we both need to get cleaned up.

INGY: Yes?

CLAIRE: You go first. Then I'm going to have a shower.

(INGY *goes.* CLAIRE *collapses on sofa. Picks up a large cushion. Puts it over her face. After a few seconds* HUGH *puts his head round the door.*)

HUGH: Has she gone?

CLAIRE: In the bathroom.

HUGH: Listen, I think I made a mistake.

CLAIRE: What?

HUGH: About Ingy.

CLAIRE: It's too late.

HUGH: She's already moved in?

CLAIRE: I've already told her.

HUGH: But . . .

CLAIRE: She's in a hell of a state. I can't suddenly tell her it's off.

(HUGH *sits down, pretends to strangle himself. Giggles.* CLAIRE *ignores him.* WILL *comes back in wearing overcoat and scarf, carrying grip and parcel.*)

Where are you going?

WILL: To Gateshead. To my aunt's.

CLAIRE: Why?

WILL: I need to think . . .

CLAIRE: You can think here.

WILL: No.

116

(*Gives* CLAIRE *the parcel.*)
I got you this yesterday.
(CLAIRE *opens it. Tweed jacket, chic. Puts it on.*)
It isn't new.

CLAIRE: It's lovely. Thanks.
(*She kisses* WILL. *Then starts to throw out the contents of the grip.*)

WILL: What are you doing?

CLAIRE: I don't know what's wrong with you at the moment. But, whatever it is, you're not going to walk out just like that. You're going to stay here and fight it out. Then if you finally decide you want to run off to Suffolk and build boats or whatever it is you secretly crave, you can. But first you've got a responsibility to me, and to the other people in the branch, and to the other people in the party. You've got a responsibility to the political views I believe you still hold. Because you know what recession and unemployment did to your father and your grandfather and it's *their* grave you'll be dancing on. And yes, I *am* going to turn down the tour. But can you see us staying together if I went away for four months?
(CLAIRE *goes out, picking up her bath towel as she goes.* WILL *stands in a debris of clothes, a cheap paperback, a copy of* Penthouse, *shaving gear.*)

WILL: If I don't get out of this party I'll go fucking mad.

HUGH: If I don't get out of this *flat*, I'll go fucking mad.

WILL: Fancy a game of bar billiards, lunchtime?

HUGH: (*Raising cut hand*) One hand tied behind me back.
(INGY *comes back in.*)

INGY: Hugh, I've been meaning to say . . . In this period, it's very important not to have any illegal drugs in the house.
(HUGH, *mock innocent expression.*)
It's not that the party is against this on moral grounds, but if this flat was raided and a connection was made through Claire, or Will, or me . . . you know, with the League – well, you know what happens if the papers get hold of this. In the eyes of the working class, all Trotskyists become drug fiends. You know, for example, the papers don't

bother that we're not a terrorist organization. And they call these terrorists Marxists, that have no practical connection with socialism at all.

WILL: Well. I'm glad you're feeling a bit perkier, Ingy.

INGY: You do understand this, Hugh?

HUGH: I'm not very interested in drugs, Ingy. But I do sometimes play baseball with some American friends in Hyde Park.

INGY: That's OK. Just tell them to get the hell out of Cambodia.

WILL: They just did.

HUGH: See, she told them.

(INGY *laughs, relaxes.* HUGH *goes to her and puts his arms round her. She tolerates this.*)

You're human, Ingy, you're human!

WILL: Aye well, when you build the revolutionary party, you have to embrace all kinds of tendencies.

(*Enter* ARNIE. '*Outward-bound' clothes, fur-lined anorak, heavy boots. Rubbing hands. A big, honest man.*)

ARNIE: Morning, comrades. All happening then, eh? There's complete traffic chaos out there. Have you tried cooking your breakfast this morning? No chance. It took me half an hour to boil a kettle this morning on our gas ring. Hospital ancillaries out tomorrow. So don't get ill, Hugh. Actually he doesn't look too good, does he?

HUGH: How did you get in?

(ARNIE *holds up a key.*)

Does anybody *not* have a key to this flat?

ARNIE: Got anything to eat? I'm starving. I've been up all night printing Tory propaganda in Fleet Street. Doesn't half give you an appetite.

WILL: I'll have a look.

(WILL *goes out.*)

ARNIE: When are you going to join us, Hugh? Better make sure you're on the right side when the time comes. I tell you, the working class are really on the move. I've just been selling the paper down Fulham Power Station. Shifted the lot. No problem. Christ, look at all these books. Have you read 'em all, Hugh?

HUGH: One time or another.

ARNIE: Ayayay! My old man's only read two books in his life. The Communist Manifesto and *The Carpetbaggers*. Seriously. He thoroughly disagrees with the Manifesto and he's read *The Carpetbaggers* thirty-three times. Have you seen *The Assassination of Trotsky*? Don't bother. He spends the whole film playing with a lot of rabbits. No mention of the *political* struggle in exile. Just a sweet old man and a load of bunnies. And nowhere does it state the truth, namely that Trotsky was murdered by Joseph Stalin with the help of provocateurs in his own household. And we know who they were too!
(*He's walking restlessly about the room, examining things, friendly*. HUGH *smiles, letting him talk*, INGY *wary, in the background*.)

ARNIE: See the National Theatre are planning a play about us.

HUGH: Don't tell me. Olivier as Jimmy Mulroy?

ARNIE: It's easy to sneer. It's a sign of the times. It may look like the bourgeois theatre playing radical chic, but it also has its opposite, somebody somewhere is trying to come to grips with these questions. You ought to get stuck in yourself, stead of translating all those Stalinist jingles. Or whatever it is you do. Russian poetry!

HUGH: There aren't any Trotskyists writing in Russian.

ARNIE: This is true. (*At the bookshelf*.) Novels . . . novels . . . novels. What's this? Marcuse! Lies, lies, lies. How to prepare a whole generation of radicals for disillusionment. Ay, ay, ay. Trouble with you intellectuals is, as soon as things start hotting up you go to ground. Turn down the central heating, start popping pills . . . It's all a big sulk because you haven't been invited to the dance.

HUGH: You think the rail strike's going to turn into a general strike? Come on.

ARNIE: Nah! They'll settle! Leadership's rotten. As soon as they start on these one day stoppages, you know the executive is digging in. But we'll see some action before the year's out, I'll tell you. You want to join this branch, Hugh. You'll have a soft time here, they're all actors. Apart from Ingy, she'll sort you out, if she hasn't already. We've got some quite nice little charmers in the League. It's always been like that. Even before we got kicked out of the Labour party. I don't know why.

HUGH: It's because you've got the biggest cocks.

ARNIE: Something like that. I tell you we work hard though. I was back home at seven this morning. Got me old man up and off to work. He's got a bit of a drink problem so it isn't easy. Then off out again on a sale. This bloody rail strike's fucked us up, too. We've got to get the papers round by road and now the second transit's got a fucked up clutch. So I've got about an hour to find someone with a car who'll do the northern deliveries.

(*He notices the pile of last night's party newspaper.*)

What's this lot doing here? Is this the locals? Who's supposed to shift these. (*To* INGY.) You?

INGY: No, well, I just deliver them here this week and Will is supposed to be doing them.

ARNIE: Yeah, but they're here, aren't they?

INGY: Yeah.

ARNIE: And so are you. So shift them. There are comrades who rely on getting their paper every morning. They're not going to think much of an organization that can't deliver a newspaper. It's the very core of our work.

INGY: Yes, but . . .

ARNIE: I haven't time to argue about this. We'll bring this up at a meeting, in case anybody has any doubts. Shift them.

(WILL *comes in with a beef sandwich for* ARNIE. INGY *glares at* WILL *as she goes out past him with the papers.* ARNIE *gives* WILL *a guarded look as he takes the sandwich, nothing more.*)

Fantastic. You've saved my life. I'd better enjoy this, hadn't I? Never know when you're going to see a piece of beef next. Now then William, where can we find a motor? One of our vans is sick and the comrades in Bootle are going to go into retreat if we don't get them some newspapers. I'm going to get them round if we have to do it on a hundred mopeds.

HUGH: I'll do them, if you like.

WILL: Hang on . . .

ARNIE: (*Sharply*) Any objections?

WILL: No . . .

ARNIE: You've got a car?

HUGH: Outside the front door.

ARNIE: OK. I'll give you the route.

HUGH: Is it far?

ARNIE: It's all written down here, but I'll run you through it quickly. M1 to Birmingham. Drop at New Street Station, you're looking for Danny, in a Commer van. M6, to Wolverhampton. I don't know why Birmingham can't do that. There's your contact. Then Liverpool, Lime Street; Chaz in a Viva. John at Manchester Central, he'll be by the Polyphoto. Can't help you in Leeds, because they haven't decided who's going out yet, but it's a big drop there because Yorkshire branch have to do the North East.

WILL: Bad luck Yorkshire.

ARNIE: Then, Barnsley, Sheffield, Nottingham and home, James, and don't spare the horses. Can you follow all that? It's all written down here, look. Barnsley's a private house, it's a miner. I don't know if you'll catch him in. It depends how long you take and what shift he's on. Take 'em round the back if not. That's what I did last time. Now you have to get down to the press and get loaded up. That's the address. Make sure you've got a bundle for each drop. You'll recognize Jim round there 'cos he's been here before now. All right then?

HUGH: Seems quite straightforward.

ARNIE: You'll see England, my old china.

(*Pause.* WILL *amazed.* HUGH *glances at the route again.*)

You've saved me a lot of bother.

(HUGH *picks up his coat.*)

Is that old Porsche yours?

HUGH: Yes.

ARNIE: The 356?

HUGH: Yes.

ARNIE: You want to watch it. Jimmy Dean got killed in one of those.

HUGH: It's the same one.

(*Goes to hall door. Turns with a grin to* WILL.)

See ya.

(*Goes.* CLAIRE *comes in. Towel round her head.*)

CLAIRE: Where was golden boy rushing off to?

ARNIE: Oh, he's just doing a little job for us.

CLAIRE: He's not doing a paper sale?

ARNIE: No, he's just wanging some papers round the north of England for us.

WILL: Probably the last we'll see of him.

CLAIRE: (*To* ARNIE) I don't believe you.

ARNIE: I remember you, when you thought a flying picket was a fence with wings.

CLAIRE: (*Ignoring the joke*) The hours I've spent working on that boy. I don't believe it!

ARNIE: It's a political lesson. People are coming to us from all sorts of strange directions.

WILL: I know, but . . .

ARNIE: And if anybody needs a political lesson at the moment, it's you. (*Turns to* CLAIRE.) I was down the press this morning, and Jimmy was there watching the papers come off, as is his wont – 'They never said we'd get a daily paper, but look at us now . . .', you know what he's like, and he said, apropos of nothing, that he'd heard you were doing a tour.

CLAIRE: How did he hear that? *I've* only just found out.

ARNIE: I don't know, but he knew. He said to tell you he thought it was a good idea. Make money. Get famous.

CLAIRE: That's amazing.

ARNIE: Er, you don't have to be completely idle while you're away. You can look up a few people for us.

CLAIRE: That's fantastic but, I'd sort of decided not to go. I didn't realize . . .

ARNIE: Obviously people must be able to work . . .

CLAIRE: I don't know what to do now.

ARNIE: I'm going to get a couple of hours' kip.

(*Goes to the door.*)

He's right. You should do it.

(*Pause.*)
Don't worry. Will can do enough party work for both of
you.
(*Grins. Goes.* WILL *and* CLAIRE *stare at each other across the
room. Slow fade. Music fade up. The Roches, 'The Hammond
Song'. To black.*)

SCENE 3

*13 December 1973. Early evening. Lights grow. As before, except
piano has more of Claire's music and papers on it, everywhere. Dark
outside, all lights in room on.* BUFFO *sits reading the late* Standard,
hysterical headline. CLAIRE *in, carrying two boxes of candles. Trims
them with a kitchen knife and fits them into various places.*

BUFFO: Hope you don't mind me hanging around like this.
CLAIRE: (*Coolly*) No, not at all.
BUFFO: Eskimos not pinched all supplies?
CLAIRE: Candles you can get. Food, forget it.
BUFFO: I keep meeting a *Jew* on the stairs. In mountaineering
   clothes. Who is he?
   (CLAIRE *ignores this. Shoves a candle into a scooped out hollow
   in Heath's head.* BUFFO *glances at her, goes back to the paper.*)
   Any idea when Hugh'll be back?
CLAIRE: For a meal, he said.
BUFFO: Not worth waiting then.
CLAIRE: I'll give him a message.
BUFFO: Doesn't seem to work nowadays.
CLAIRE: He's very busy at the moment.
   (*Goes upstage behind* BUFFO.)
   How's Tod?
BUFFO: He had his op today. I'm going to ring in a few
   minutes.
CLAIRE: Will he be out for Xmas?
BUFFO: It's only a varicose vein. He should be out by the
   weekend. I hope so anyway. I don't like my own company
   much.
CLAIRE: I'd noticed.

BUFFO: Look . . . I'm sorry.

CLAIRE: No, no. *I'm* sorry. I didn't mean that.

BUFFO: Better be off, anyway. Just tell him, I've finally found those old *New Yorkers*. Maybe I'll bring them down.

CLAIRE: No, look. It's after six. Have a drink before you go.
(*Said without conviction. She carries on putting the candles round.* BUFFO *thinks for a second.*)

BUFFO: All right, I will. Thanks.
(CLAIRE *places a candle, rather deliberately in a wine bottle. Goes to pour him a gin.* BUFFO *looks over at Heath.*)
You know I feel quite sympatico with our friend over there.

CLAIRE: Really? Why?

BUFFO: Both the same age. Well, almost.
(*Pause.* CLAIRE *mixes the gin.*)
Both stagger from one disaster to the next. Both . . .
(CLAIRE *smiles, still upstage.* BUFFO *glances back at the* Evening Standard.)
What a year for death. Piccasso, Coward, Tolkien.
(*Pause.*)
Compton Mackenzie.
(*Longer pause.*)
Nancy Mitford.
(CLAIRE *behind* BUFFO, *with drink. Hands it to him over his shoulder.*)

CLAIRE: Salvador Allende.
(*In very close.*)
How are you feeling in yourself, Buffo?

BUFFO: Oh, not too bad. Who?

CLAIRE: Forget it.

BUFFO: I could never despise anybody for their political opinions.

CLAIRE: It's a great temptation, though, isn't it?

BUFFO: Did you know I was drummed out of the Civil Service for being a queer? I tell you, that oik Vassal's got a lot to answer for.

CLAIRE: I did. I mean, I'd heard.

BUFFO: The problem with being the son of someone famous is, you spend the first half of your life trying to live up to it, and the second half trying to live down having failed.

CLAIRE: I'm sorry I haven't been very sociable. I've got a lot on my mind at the moment.

BUFFO: Quite understand. I slope around horribly at the moment. (*Pause.*) You don't talk about yourself much.

CLAIRE: My parents are separated. My mother wants me to spend Xmas in Shropshire, my father wants me to spend Xmas in the Dordogne. The party wants me to spend Xmas in London.

BUFFO: Who'll win?

CLAIRE: I'm daddy's girl. But it will be terrible. It's always the same. I get drunk and read endless old copies of *Paris Match* and have rows. 'Enfin, la Guerre Algérie est fini.'

BUFFO: I hear your tour was a success and now you're going to be on the box.

CLAIRE: BBC 2. After everyone's gone to bed. My agent's providing me with bodyguards. So I don't talk politics to the camera crew.

BUFFO: Tod gets very excited. When you're practising down here. He won't let me talk. How can you cope with all this *and* the *putsch*?

CLAIRE: Aha! The iron fist in the woolly cardigan. This is difficult. I don't really want to talk politics with you, Buffo.

BUFFO: What a bloody insult. I couldn't care less anyway. I'm completely ignorant about politics and I'm proud of it.

CLAIRE: OK. Let's leave it.

BUFFO: I've been so bloody happy this last year. I don't know why. First fifty years of my life, a complete wash out.

CLAIRE: You both ought to have a treat once in a while. Go to Morocco, or something.

BUFFO: Last time I left London for more than half a day. I was arrested. That was in 1958. We go boating sometimes. Richmond to Hampton Court. Rat and Mole. Sod Morocco, I say.

(*Phone rings.* CLAIRE *doesn't pick it up immediately, but* BUFFO *gets up, prepares to go.*)

Tell Hugh . . . no don't bother. I'll come up later. D'you know it's six months since I had a proper conversation with him?

CLAIRE: If you need anything . . .

BUFFO: All kitted up, thanks. Got a couple of birds out of the freezer for the weekend. *La Grande Bouffe*!

(BUFFO *goes out.* CLAIRE *picks up phone, settles back.*)

CLAIRE: Hello? Yes, I got the message this morning. Yes, I've been on the phone rather a lot. Can you tell me, what kind of an interview you want? . . . No, what I mean is, I don't want to leave politics completely out of it, so if you're prepared . . . Well, you see, everybody knows I'm a member of the RSP so why bother to be coy about it? . . . Yes, it's changed . . . *RSP*. It was, yes. I'll explain all that. You came to the pageant, didn't you? Yes, it was. It was amazing. Listen, we have this enormous drive on at the moment. To get funds . . . Yes, I know . . .

(WILL *comes in. Donkey jacket, over overalls, canvas bag; watches* CLAIRE.)

Well, we're the only principled opposition to the Tories in this period. It's incredible how strong the opposition to Stage Three is . . . No, I'll talk about music till the cows come home. Could you give us a donation? I can collect it when I come . . . How much? . . . Come on, you can afford more than that on your salary . . . All right, we'll discuss it then.

(*Puts down receiver. Claire's attitude to* WILL *is very watchful and reserved throughout.*)

You look tired.

WILL: It's hard work in the motor industry.

CLAIRE: You're supposed to finish at lunch time.

WILL: You won't believe it. We had a play. Ironic, eh?

CLAIRE: Oh no, what? Agitprop?

WILL: Sort of. There were two actors there I knew.

CLAIRE: Who?

WILL: John Craggs . . .

CLAIRE: He's IMG.

WILL: They *say* they're not affiliated to any political party.

CLAIRE: John Craggs has an *Open University degree* in revisionism. He thinks Tariq Ali is an important political philosopher.

126

WILL: I know, I know. Well, anyway . . .

CLAIRE: Didn't you do anything about it?

WILL: It was quite witty. A cut above the usual agitprop stuff.

CLAIRE: What about politics?

WILL: Not much. It was a history of Fords.

CLAIRE: What were they trying to *do* for God's sake?

WILL: I think they were trying to say Capitalism Is A Bad Thing.

CLAIRE: How did they work *that* out?

WILL: It went down all right. Popular theme. Some liked it, some didn't. Some went home. An old CPer stood up and said, 'We don't want a lot of students coming down here and telling us how to run our strikes.' Somebody pointed out that we weren't actually *on* strike, so he shut up. Craggs said, 'We're not students, actually. I've been a working actor for eleven years.' Somebody shouted from the back, 'You haven't learnt much!'

CLAIRE: Did you ask them what their political position was?

WILL: I did.

CLAIRE: And . . .

WILL: It's difficult. It's embarrassing . . .

CLAIRE: Listen, you're in the thick of a political struggle . . .

WILL: Craggs came up to me afterwards, with a smirk and said, 'I see the RSP are trying to build a base amongst the proletariat at last.'

CLAIRE: Cunt. What did you say?

WILL: I told him I was doing it because I wanted a steady job with regular wages.

CLAIRE: That's not the only reason!

WILL: He thought there'd been some strings pulled to get me a skilled job. I had to tell him, I only stick on the Ford badges and polish them up. That's called humiliation in any language. I don't want to talk about it any more. I'm tired.

CLAIRE: But what kind of opposition did you pose to these questions?

WILL: I'm tired.

CLAIRE: There's a State of Emergency, Will.

WILL: I'm tired.

CLAIRE: These people are dangerous.

WILL: John Craggs isn't dangerous. He's too wet. He's lucky I didn't break his jaw.

CLAIRE: They're dangerous! They divert the working class away from politics. They say, 'We're not fighting the Tory Government, we're fighting capitalism.' It's irrelevant to them that the Tories are the one and only political instrument of capitalism in this country. What do they want? A workers' government based on the Trade Unions or something silly like that? Ignore the century of working-class struggle that went into building the Labour Party? Keep demands to a minimum so that the majority will always agree? Sheer bloody pragmatism. And the more serious the political situation becomes, the more they attempt to stifle any talk about politics among the working class. It's incred –

(*Blackout. Both swear.* WILL *strikes a match, lights a candle. He hands the box over to* CLAIRE. *Candles lit during the next minute.*)

CLAIRE: What time did the play finish?

WILL: I don't know. There was the discussion . . . Why?

CLAIRE: I was just interested to, you know . . . I wondered how long it was.

WILL: I dunno. How long's a piece of string. . . ?

(INGY *comes in.*)

INGY: Can I have a candle?

CLAIRE: I didn't know you were in.

INGY: I was reading.

WILL: (*Cynically*) No doubt devouring 'The Tasks of the Fourth International'.

INGY: *The Lady of the Lake.*

CLAIRE: Arnie rang. He wants to know if you can speak at a youth meeting in Wandsworth tomorrow night.

INGY: Why didn't he tell me at lunchtime? I saw him then. It's completely stupid. Thanks.

(INGY *takes a candle and goes.*)

WILL: No love lost there.

CLAIRE: She found out that he ran away last year.

WILL: Loss of political respect. I didn't know that.

128

CLAIRE: During the last miners' strike. I think his nerve must
have gone. He just disappeared off the face of the earth.
Somebody told me he spent all his savings and tried to start
a small printing business in Corby. But he couldn't make it
pay. Have you ever been round to his flat? He lives with his
old man. It's a fifties council block. Two rooms. The lifts
smell of piss. And every morning Arnie and his old man go
to work together to Fulham Power Station. Arnie stands
outside the gate with the paper and his old man shouts
political insults at him as he goes through. Could *you* take
that?

WILL: What's wrong?

CLAIRE: What do you mean?

WILL: I don't know. There's something up with you. You
haven't done a moody like this since I threw your valium
down the lav.
(*Sharp stone cracks against the window.* WILL *goes over, looks
out.*)

CLAIRE: Who is it?

WILL: Can't see.

CLAIRE: Why don't they use the bell?

WILL: I'll go down.
(WILL *goes out.* CLAIRE *goes to the telephone, picks up the
receiver, doesn't dial. Listens for a few seconds.*)

CLAIRE: I don't know who you are. Or in what dull little police
office you're sitting. But I strongly advise you to go home.
Because you won't hear anything remotely interesting.
(*She slams down the receiver. Voices coming up the stairs,
laughing.* WILL's *voice.* 'Osgood's rubbish.' ARNIE's *voice,*
'Did you see that goal on Saturday? Amazing positioning.
Amazing!' WILL's *voice,* 'Positioning? He'd been standing
there since half time!' ARNIE *in, followed by* WILL.)

ARNIE: Evening, comrades. All happening, eh? I've been
standing outside Shepherd's Bush Metropolitan. Fuckin'
freezing. Sold every copy in half an hour. Another couple of
weeks of this and we might persuade the miners' executive
to get their fingers out.
(*Rubs his hands gleefully. Indicates the dark room.*)

Isn't this wonderful? My old feller's doing. Bless his heart, he hates industrial action. Any chance of a bite to eat? I'm starving. Anything'll do.

(CLAIRE *smiles, goes out.*)

My old man's a miserable old customer. Anybody'd think they were on strike. They've only banned out-of-hours work. I told him the Tory hawks were trying to get Heath to withdraw social security benefits to strikers. He nearly jumped out the window. He's got nothing to worry about. His bloody union are going to settle this week, I'll bet you a gorilla. Leadership's petrified in case anybody might think they're in collusion with the miners. Mind you, Heath's made a mistake shoving Whitelaw in the front line. He's like a balding Isthmian League centre back trying to mark Dennis Law. How's the job?

WILL: Can't complain. How's yours?

ARNIE: It's better than working for Rothermere. We've got a new offset litho. I reckon our photo reproduction beats anybody's. Look at that.

WILL: Got your work and your politics into line.

ARNIE: We keep Jimmy on his toes though. We've got a twenty-five per cent claim in at the moment.

(CLAIRE *back in with a pork pie. Throws it to* ARNIE.)

Thanks.

CLAIRE: How are we going to afford it?

ARNIE: Increase the monthly fund. This is good. Better enjoy it. Never know when you're going to see a piece of pork next. Pork this evening, this morning I married a gentile. My old lady'd turn, if she knew.

(*Pause.* ARNIE *munches.*)

I came round to see my wife, actually. Is she in?

CLAIRE: Er . . .

ARNIE: Ingy. Immigration office is on the war path. We discussed it with a couple of other comrades. It seemed to be the best thing to do. In the circumstances.

CLAIRE: She didn't say anything.

ARNIE: Well, she wouldn't, would she? I suppose it's what you call a marriage of convenience. There's nothing . . . *you* know. Did you pass on the message?

CLAIRE: She said she'd do it.

ARNIE: I thought I'd come round anyway. You know what she's like.

WILL: She's in her room. Working very hard on some theory.

CLAIRE: Perhaps you might go and tell her Arnie's here.

WILL: Your servant.

(WILL *goes out*.)

CLAIRE: I'm so glad you turned up. I've been going out of my mind. I think Will's spying on us.

ARNIE: *Spying?*

CLAIRE: He's not straight. He's been seeing an American, he tells lies about his movements.

ARNIE: Who'd employ him as a spy? He couldn't deceive anyone.

CLAIRE: Roy Johnson bumped into him by mistake. He thinks this guy is connected with the CIA. He's seen him before. They're trying to check up on him.

ARNIE: It's possible. Just. But . . .

CLAIRE: We've got masses of evidence that the CIA have stepped up their activities in Britain. Exactly what happened in Chile. You've got a sudden move to the left, a political crisis. Their technique is to infiltrate the left parties and use *agents provocateurs* to get names and addresses . . .

(WILL *comes back in*.)

WILL: She's just finishing a chapter. She's locked the door.

ARNIE: Look, I won't disturb her. It's probably the only time the kid gets to herself.

(ARNIE *rises to go*. CLAIRE *stands*.)

CLAIRE: No, no. I'll go and have a word with her.

(CLAIRE *goes out*. ARNIE *embarrassed*.)

ARNIE: How're you doing anyway, chief?

WILL: All right, you know . . .

ARNIE: Hard work, is it?

WILL: It's not so much that it's hard, you know . . .

ARNIE: Haven't seen so much of you lately.

WILL: What d'you mean?

ARNIE: Haven't seen you out, you know, with the paper.

WILL: I'm working half nights.

ARNIE: You go to your union meetings?

WILL: I go to my union meetings.

ARNIE: It has to be a very principled struggle in this period. You're going to meet this whole rag-bag of centrists trying to set up diversions – feminism, gay power, dog power, work-ins, sit-ins. It's not like Equity – you've got a very basic struggle there, against a union which can't decide if it wants to be a union or not. But where you are now, it's on a much higher level. The stakes are much higher. But the right policies don't necessarily make you popular. It's much simpler to keep your mouth shut, than put forward a maximum demand like Nationalization and be jeered at. It's much simpler sometimes to run for cover.

WILL: I've heard tell some people disappear completely from time to time.

ARNIE: (*Without a blink*) True, true. It's a tough discipline. It has to become your life. No half measures.

WILL: Aye, well . . .

ARNIE: But you know which side you're on, don't you?

WILL: Yes, I know which side I'm on.

ARNIE: You can't have it both ways. You can't have friends outside the party.

WILL: No?

(CLAIRE *comes in again, with* INGY. INGY *is transformed. Make-up, no glasses.*)

INGY: I had a bit of a migraine. I'm all right now.

WILL: Congratulations! Let's celebrate! Let's have a party!
(*Goes to portable cassette player, puts on a record, rhythm and blues, not too appropriate.*)
Why not?

INGY: Why not? I feel like being stupid.

ARNIE: We can't really celebrate. It isn't a *real* marriage.

WILL: Scotch or gin. That's all there is. Anybody not want Scotch?

INGY: My sister got married in Hamburg. There were six hundred guests.

WILL: (*To* CLAIRE) Knock it back.

INGY: It was terrible. They drank two thousand litres of beer.

WILL: (*To* INGY) Knock it back.

INGY: My step-father had to get a bank loan.

WILL: (*To* ARNIE) Knock it back.

ARNIE: German workers are very thirsty. Too many productivity deals.

WILL: (*To himself*) Knock it back.
(*He drains his Scotch in one, and pours another.* INGY *has put hers quietly aside.*)

ARNIE: Here's to . . .

WILL: Friendship.

ARNIE: I can't think of anything to drink a toast to.

INGY: (*Quietly*) Don't you say, 'The Happy Couple'?

ARNIE: No, *we* don't.

CLAIRE: (*To* INGY) Did you ever find your bag?

INGY: No, it's gone for good. Better that way. Forget it.
(WILL *turns the music up louder. Goes over to* CLAIRE *puts an arm round her.*)

WILL: D'you want to dance, beautiful?

CLAIRE: I don't feel like it, thanks.

WILL: Please yourself. Hey! Maybe we can go out and eat later. What do you say?

ARNIE: Why not?

INGY: It's not possible, Arnie, we have to . . .

WILL: It's OK! I've just got paid.
(*Pulls out a roll of fivers.*)
Look! Capitalism is still flourishing! Tarar! Tarar!
(*Phone rings.*)
Come and dance with me, Ingy.

INGY: No, I . . .
(WILL *picks up the phone and grabs* INGY's *hand at the same time. He pulls her up.*)

WILL: I won't take no for an answer, Ingy. Hello?
(*He pulls her into a clinch, cradling the phone.*)
Who? No. Hang on a minute.
(*Waves the phone at* CLAIRE, *carries on jiggling with* INGY.)
It's for you.

CLAIRE: (*Taking the phone*) Hello . . .

WILL: You can't fool me, Ingy. I know you were Frankfurt area ballroom dance champion for 1968.

INGY: Oh, yeah, it's true.

CLAIRE: (*Looking at* WILL, *into the phone*) It's a bit difficult to talk at the moment. Hang on a minute.

(*She takes the telephone through into Hugh's bedroom and shuts the door.* WILL *and* INGY *carry on dancing for a bit.* ARNIE *out of it.*)

INGY: I still have a bit of a headache.

(WILL *lets her go.*)

WILL: What's going on? I'm getting paranoid.

(WILL *goes over to cassette player, turns it down,* ARNIE *sensitive to the situation.*)

ARNIE: D'you want to hear my party piece?

(*Pause.*)

The Order of Precedence. Know it off by heart.

INGY: What's that?

ARNIE: Hang on. I've got to prepare for this.

(*Takes a big swig of whisky. Deep breath.*)

Right. Here goes. The sovereign. The Prince Philip, Duke of Edinburgh. The Prince of Wales, the Prince Andrew, the Prince Edward. The Duke of Gloucester. Archbishop of Canterbury. Lord High Chancellor. Archbishop of York. The Prime Minister. Lord President of the Council. Speaker of the House of Commons. Lord Privy Seal. High Commissioners of Commonwealth Countries and Ambassadors of Foreign States. Dukes according to their patents of creation: One, of England; Two, of Scotland; Three, of Great Britain; Four, of Ireland; Five, those created since the Union. Ministers and Envoys. Eldest sons of Dukes of Royal Blood. Marquesses in the same order as Dukes. Dukes' eldest sons. Earls, in the same order as Dukes. Younger sons of Dukes of Royal Blood. Marquesses' eldest sons. Dukes' younger sons. Viscounts in the same order as Dukes. Earls' eldest sons. Marquesses' younger sons. Bishops of London, Durham and Winchester. All other English Bishops, according to the seniority of Consecration. Secretaries of State if of the degree of a Baron. Barons, in the same order as Dukes. Treasurers of Her Majesty's Household. Comptroller of HM's Household. Vice-Chamberlain of HM's Household. Secretaries of State under the degree of Baron. Viscounts' eldest sons. Earls' younger sons. Barons' eldest sons. Knights of the Garter if commoners. Privy Councillors if of no higher rank. Chancellor of the Exchequer. Chancellor of the Duchy of Lancaster. Lord Chief Justice of England. Master of the Rolls. President of the Probate Court. The Lord Justices of Appeal. Judges of the High Court. Vice-Chancellor of the County Palatinate of Lancaster. Viscounts' younger sons. Barons' younger sons. Sons of Life Peers. Baronets of either kingdom according to date of patents. Knights of the Thistle if commoners . . . aaaaah!

(ARNIE *takes another deep breath.* WILL *and* INGY *are by now on the edge of their seats, smiling and willing him on.*)

Knights Grand Cross of the Bath. Members of the Order of Merit. Knights Grand Commanders of the Star of India. Knights Grand Cross of St Michael and St George. Knights Grand Commanders of the Indian Empire. Knights Grand Cross of the Royal Victorian Order. Knights Grand Cross of the Order of the British Empire. Companions of Honour. Knights Commanders of the above orders. Knights Bachelor. Official Referees of the Supreme Court, Judges of County Courts and Judges of the Mayor's and City of London Court. Companions and Commanders e.g. CB; CSI; CMG; CIE; CVO; CBE; DSO; MVO; OBE; ISO. Eldest sons of younger sons of Peers. Baronets' eldest sons. Eldest sons of Knights in the same order as their fathers. MBE. Younger sons of the younger sons of Peers. Baronet's younger sons. Younger sons of Knights in the same order as their fathers. *Naval, Military, Air, and other Esquires by Office!*

(WILL *and* INGY *applaud.*)

Hang on I haven't finished yet. Women . . .

(CLAIRE *comes out of the bedroom off. Impassive. Has finished the call, is holding the telephone loosely, by her side. Watches from the door.*)

Women take the same rank as their husbands or as their eldest brothers; but the daughter of a Peer marrying a commoner retains her title as Lady or Honourable. Daughters of Peers rank next immediately after the wives of their elder brothers, and before their younger brothers' wives. Daughters of Peers marrying Peers of lower degree take the same order of precedency as that of their husbands; thus the daughter of a Duke marrying a Baron becomes of the rank of Baroness only, while her sisters married to commoners retain their rank and take precedence of the Baroness. Merely official rank on the husband's part does not give any similar precedence to the wife.

(ARNIE *relaxes back in the sofa, grins at* INGY, *next to him.*)
My old lady taught it to me when I was four. I've updated it a bit. We had a copy of *Whitaker's Almanac,* 1938. She wanted me to fit in. She thought my old man was the only Jew in Britain that hadn't dragged his family out of the working class. She used to shout at him, 'We're not factory people.' 'But I can't sew, Peppi!' he used to say to her. I learnt *Hymns Ancient and Modern* too. But we never had the tunes.

(CLAIRE *puts the phone down. Goes over to the piano.*)

INGY: Can I have a light?

(ARNIE *produces a lighter.* INGY *has her hand on his thigh.*
CLAIRE *plays a couple of jazz chords, blue.*)

CLAIRE: Will . . .

(*In the dark it's just possible to see* ARNIE's *hand cover* INGY's.)

WILL: What?

(CLAIRE *turns round from the piano.*)

CLAIRE: Can I have a word?

WILL: (*After a pause*) Yeah. Here you are.

(*Produces an imaginary word from his mouth and tosses it across to her.* ARNIE *puts a hand in* INGY's *hair.*)

CLAIRE: Can we go into our room, or something?

WILL: I want to stay here.

(ARNIE *and* INGY *are kissing.* WILL *is sipping Scotch, seems far away.* CLAIRE *starts to play, very loud but a clever 'big' performance.*)

CLAIRE: 'I see the church, I see the steeple,

Your hand in mine, faithful and true,
And I can hear sweet voices singing
Ave Maria! Ave Maria!
Oh, my love, my love, can this really be,
That you will walk down the aisle with me . . .'
(WILL *joins in on the second chorus, very loud.* ARNIE *and*
INGY *still kissing.* HUGH *comes in. Anorak, open-necked check
shirt, boots. Canvas bag, with copies of the paper sticking out.
Looks tougher, coarser, less relaxed. Takes in the candles.*)

HUGH: Well, I'm glad *we're* not the foolish virgins. What's
going on? A funeral?
(*He peers over towards the sofa. The lights suddenly come on.*
INGY *and* ARNIE *spring apart. Preoccupied, neither* WILL *nor*
CLAIRE *have noticed them kissing.* ARNIE, *nonchalant.*)

WILL: Not discouraged by the fact that Stalin upheld the family
as the bastion of the Socialist State, these comrades have
just got wed.

ARNIE: Yeah well, Stalin encouraged one way sleigh rides too,
comrade. But we're giving that a miss at the moment.

INGY: I was going to have to go back to Germany.
(*This is very obviously meant for* HUGH's *benefit, but he's into
himself and doesn't really hear.* CLAIRE *is going round blowing
out the candles.*)

HUGH: Congratulations . . .
(WILL *reacts to* HUGH *in amazement. Hits his head with the
heel of his hand.*
CLAIRE *is near* WILL.)

CLAIRE: Will, please . . .

WILL: I've got nothing to talk about, pet. I just want to sit here
and relax for a bit.
(HUGH *is unpacking his bag very carefully. Sorting out pages of
notes. Copies of Trotsky's* Revolution Betrayed, *Lenin's* State
and Revolution. *Speaks to* ARNIE.)

HUGH: Are you going down to the press later?

ARNIE: Yes, I'm on at ten.

HUGH: I'll give you a lift. I've got a piece for the paper on the
crisis in the British Film industry.

WILL: What bloody film industry?

HUGH: (*To* CLAIRE) I thought you were coming to the studios this afternoon?

CLAIRE: I'm sorry. I had to make some calls.

HUGH: We got through a motion to nationalize the entire fucking British film industry! Against the leadership of the union. I'm sorry you didn't come. It was a very important meeting.

CLAIRE: I've been on the phone all day. Trying to raise money for the fund.

(CLAIRE *stays calm, isn't needled.* ARNIE *has stood up.*)

ARNIE: I'm on my way. Thanks for the offer, but I want to go home first, check out the old feller. (*To* INGY, *quietly*) I might call in on my way home, in the morning.

INGY: What time?

ARNIE: Oh, 'bout five.

(INGY *grins, follows* ARNIE *to the door.*)

HUGH: See you, Arnie. Keep up the good work.

(ARNIE *and* INGY *go out.* CLAIRE *is staring at* WILL.)

WILL: What do you *want*?

CLAIRE: What do *you* want?

WILL: (*Angrily*) I want to play *Hamlet*! On a *world tour*!

HUGH: Well, unfortunately, this society stops us doing exactly what we want. We're all faced with contradictions in our lives. But it's at the point at which you translate all this confusion, through Marxist theory, into *practice* that you begin to understand the world.

(WILL *gets up and walks out of the room.* HUGH *turns his attention to* CLAIRE. *They argue, but it isn't a row – it's weary and tense.*)

I don't think you should go away for Christmas.

CLAIRE: I haven't seen my father for two years.

HUGH: How important is your family compared to the political situation? The working class is completely unprepared to take power if there's a general strike.

CLAIRE: There won't be one at Christmas.

HUGH: There are no objective grounds for saying that. You may find yourself in France not wanting to come back to a military dictatorship.

CLAIRE: You can't expect me *as an individual* to take responsibility for that.

HUGH: Pragmatically you may be right, but as a matter of principle, you're wrong. The political situation is always changing. The miners' executive are meeting *now*, right now. There is going to be a strike.

CLAIRE: I'm not going to be told what to do. I've spent four years working my tits off for socialism. *I* am going to decide when I spend a few precious days with my father.

HUGH: This is a completely individualist position. Listen to yourself. I, I, I, I.

CLAIRE: You have all the same problems. But you won't bring them out in the open. You won't *admit* them to yourself.
(WILL *comes back in, with* BUFFO. *He looks pale, and is carrying two grouse*.)

WILL: Here's Buffo. He's brought a couple of birds along.

BUFFO: They're no use to me.

CLAIRE: Is Tod all right?

BUFFO: I don't know. But he won't be back at the weekend. So. Eat well.
(*He hands the grouse to* WILL.)

HUGH: What do you do with them?

BUFFO: Pull the feathers off. Scoop out the innards. Stick 'em in the oven.
(WILL *holds them at arm's length, eyes watering*.)

CLAIRE: I thought he was having a vein removed.

BUFFO: There were complications. A blood clot. So they had to operate again. He's still out.

CLAIRE: Do you want a gin?

BUFFO: No thanks. Feel a bit queasy. I think I'll turn in.

CLAIRE: I'm sorry. I'm sorry for you.

HUGH: Is he going to be all right?

BUFFO: They reckon it's gone very well. We'll see.

HUGH: I had an uncle who lived to be eighty on a quarter of a kidney.

BUFFO: Yerse, chickens run around for miles after you've chopped their heads off.
(*Makes a move to go*.)

139

HUGH: I'll drop round tomorrow.

BUFFO: (*Doubtfully*) Yes . . .

HUGH: Honestly, I will this time . . .

BUFFO: Anyway, if they give him a pacemaker, I hope it's got its own power supply.

(*Goes.* WILL *takes a copy of Edgar Mittelholzer's* Kaywana Blood *from the bookshelf.* HUGH *turns his attention to* WILL.)

WILL: I'm going to have a quiet read.

HUGH: (*Not noticing the book*) Of course it's important to know the theory. We have to build a leadership, and if you're ambitious to lead, you've got to read the books . . .

WILL: I do understand the theory of opposites, you know.

HUGH: You've got to understand that this Tory government is trying to create the conditions for a kind of . . . Bonapartist dictatorship. They'll allow services to deteriorate and get people very frightened. They'll push the working class to the limit on wages and prices and they're going to turn round and say, 'Who's running the country?' And they're prepared to bring in the heavy boys to sort things out. You've heard of Brigadier Kitson? This man's been trained in Aden and Cyprus and God knows where in *counter-insurgency techniques*. You can bet your sweet bippy he's advising the government right now on what to do if there's a mass insurgency like a general strike. And it won't be rest homes for workers. You only have to study Germany in the late twenties. The economic conditions are very similar. And now we've got the National Front organizing, campaigning, swaggering about. The question that's being posed here is, what are you going to do about it?

CLAIRE: That's not the only question that's being posed.

WILL: What am I going to do about it?

HUGH: What are *you* going to do about this political crisis?

WILL: I don't know.

HUGH: Well let us know when you've made up your mind.

(*Pause.* HUGH *relaxes a bit.*)

WILL: OK.

CLAIRE: I really must talk to you . . .

WILL: I've made up my mind, Hugh. You're right.

(HUGH *comes across, puts an arm round* WILL's *shoulder*.)

HUGH: Maybe we can slip out for a pint later on?

(WILL *suddenly swings the brace of grouse up sharply, catching*
HUGH *neatly on the jaw. One of the birds splits, spreading
blood and offal.* HUGH *staggers back, catches hold of a
standard lamp to steady himself, but* HUGH *and the lamp lurch,
spin and keel over on to the floor.* WILL *shaking with anger,
drops the birds on the carpet.*)

WILL: I've had enough of this.

CLAIRE: (*Shouting*) *Why are you giving information to the CIA?*

WILL: WHAT!

CLAIRE: These secret meetings, Will. You've been seen. Why?
Why?

WILL: Oh, I don't believe this . . .

CLAIRE: Why?

WILL: I don't believe this is *happening*.

CLAIRE: You went on a train with an American called Walter
Holac!

WILL: Yes, to Leigh-on-sea.

CLAIRE: He's got CIA connections.

WILL: Knackers!

CLAIRE: His father was assistant editor of *Encounter*.

WILL: So what . . .

CLAIRE: Everybody knows the CIA backed *Encounter*.

HUGH: Look I'm all right. Don't worry about *me*.

CLAIRE: You meet him when you're supposed to be at work.
You lied to me about your work hours.

WILL: Who's been spying on me?

CLAIRE: Nobody.

HUGH: I don't think Wal has any connection with the CIA.
Unless he's trying to pervert the youth of the country.

WILL: What I do in my spare time is *my* business.

HUGH: He makes his money selling dope. Maybe he's joined the
dirty tricks department. . . ?

WILL: But since you seem to be interested, I'll tell you. Walter
Holac owns an east coast sailing barge. It's moored at
Canvey Island. It needs restoring. He wants to sell it. I've
been saving up for a down payment on a marine mortgage.

We've been trying to negotiate a price.

(*He goes out.* HUGH *is now completely relaxed, suddenly out of himself.* CLAIRE *giving nothing away.* HUGH *laughs, trying to wipe away bits of grouse.*)

HUGH: I think I swallowed something very nasty.

CLAIRE: Let's have a look.

HUGH: Poor bastard. We discovered his tunnel.

CLAIRE: There's a little cut. I'll clean it up.

(*She goes to her bag and gets out some Kleenex and witch-hazel.*)

HUGH: Maybe there's a whole load of CIA operatives going round offering sailing boats to militants, in the hope they'll call off the struggle? It's an idea.

CLAIRE: Come on.

HUGH: Mummy.

(CLAIRE *cleans the cut, leaning over* HUGH.)

HUGH: You've got little downy hairs on the nape of your neck.

(CLAIRE *draws back, but only slightly. Lights fade to black. Music over. Joni Mitchell, 'Down to You':*

'Everything comes and goes,

Marked by lovers and styles of clothes . . .

Things that you held high

And told yourself were true

Lost or changing as the days come down to you . . .')

INTERVAL

ACT II

SCENE 4

*8 January 1974. In preset lights, Joni Mitchell, 'People's Parties'.
Cross fade into Roland Kirk on stereo as lights to black.*

*Fade up on room, as before. Midnight. Now, much less tidy,
books and papers everywhere. Heath model almost completely
covered up. Empty cartons of take-away meals. Evidence of much
activity. The piano is closed and the music is stacked neatly.
Bedroom door is open. Light on.* CLAIRE *comes out of the bedroom,
in a large pullover, nothing else. Goes over to the round table,
searches among the papers.*

CLAIRE: It was in the *Standard*. We had one somewhere . . .
  (*Finds copy.*)
  Found it. I'll read it to you.
  (*Wanders back, towards bedroom.*)
  'As the nation's factories, shops and businesses turn off
  electricity to conserve coal stocks, electrical equipment in
  the homes of laid-off workers is switched on . . . Take Cut
  'n Dry, a small salon in Bride Lane, City. The water supply
  is heated by gas and Mr Saunders finds he can manage
  without using direct heating as the constant use of
  hairdryers keeps the salon warm. But since the government
  demands that Cut 'n Dry remains closed for all but three
  hours each day, the hairdressers spend either the whole
  morning or the whole afternoon at home . . . When I talked
  to them I discovered that between them they had used in
  their homes, five lights, four 2kW heaters, five electric
  kettles, three electric cookers, one washing machine, two
  vacuum cleaners, two hairdryers, three record players, two
  tape recorders and one iron. This works out at more than
  five times as much electricity as they would have used in the
  salon.'
  (*Leans against the door.*)
  Proves it, doesn't it. Danger is, the situation's so bizarre,
  that nobody believes it's actually happening.
  (*Throws the paper back on the table.*)

Anyway, you spoke brilliantly. I've never heard you speak like that before. I mean, it's a small step from, 'It can't happen here', to 'It isn't happening here.'

(*She laughs.*)

What are you doing? Put it away.

(*Goes back across the room. Collects her bag, starts to go back. Enter* HUGH *from the hall with a tray of mugs.* CLAIRE *pulls her sweater down.*)

CLAIRE: You didn't mind moving bedrooms, did you?

HUGH: No, no.

(WILL *comes out of the bedroom. T-shirt, bare feet, zipping up Levis.*)

CLAIRE: I'm sure it'll help you sleep.

WILL: On your own tonight? I haven't seen you without a lass for weeks.

HUGH: Sorry to disappoint you.

CLAIRE: Yes, I'm getting a bit *tired*, love, of having tear-stained recruits from the actors' branch crying on my shoulder and threatening to join the Communist Party because you're not taking them home tonight.

WILL: He hasn't changed, you know.

HUGH: Nobody's offered.

(*Sits down.*)

Sorry I missed you tonight. I was back in time. I just forgot. One of the youth in Fulham had his head kicked in, shook me up a bit.

CLAIRE: Doesn't matter. I hate watching myself.

HUGH: I know. but . . .

CLAIRE: Wait till I get some good songs, eh. I wish I could clear my skull and start writing. Ah, Lady Day, they all just stuck to her. But I dunno, do they *connect* now, they're just ghosts – women fucked up, yearning. Too beautiful and remote for me, I don't do well as a siren. Joni's OK. She's a poet, but she's precious. What's it's like to be a privileged white rock singer, having affairs with other privileged rock singers? I wish Randy Newman had been a woman. I wonder if I look good on the box? That's all I care about, really.

(*All relaxed, drinking.*)

WILL: Do you know when I first met him?

CLAIRE: Don't tell me, I don't want to know.

HUGH: He always does this to me. No one's interested, Will.

CLAIRE: Change the subject.

WILL: And another thing. Next show the party puts on, I'm not playing any more *backsliders*. Number of hours of party work I've put in this month, I reckon I'm due for something more heroic. It always has to be *me* that goes cap in hand to the boss, or embezzles the union funds. And if this Russian Revolution show comes off I am *not* playing the Tsar, Rasputin or *fucking Anastasia*.

HUGH: Someone has to play the minor roles in history.

CLAIRE: You just don't look like Trotsky.

WILL: Anyway *he'd* been doing his Eastern Mystic bit . . .

CLAIRE: Change the subject.

HUGH: Er . . .

WILL: Only he got one of the gurus George Harrison didn't want . . .

CLAIRE: Quick, quick.

HUGH: I can't think . . .

CLAIRE: Come on, this is boring . . .

WILL: He was the only bankrupt guru in Hyderabad.

HUGH: Did you know I was going to do a new translation of the 'Internationale'?

WILL: Are you?

HUGH: Yep.

WILL: Seriously.

HUGH: Well have you *heard* the one we use? It's terrible.

CLAIRE: I don't think it's terrible.

HUGH: 'Arise ye starvelings from your slumber, arise ye criminals of want . . .'

CLAIRE: I like it.

HUGH: Best of a bad lot. Do you know 'Arise ye prisoners of starvation, arise ye wretched of the earth . . .' very bland . . .

WILL: (*Laughing*) I first met *him* . . .

HUGH: You won't believe it, anyway.

CLAIRE: Where?

WILL: On a cargo boat in the Bay of Bengal.

HUGH: We were both being sick over the same rail.

WILL: We got back to Cairo together. Then he ditched me.

HUGH: I found an American girl who paid for my hotel. Tough shit.

WILL: It took me five weeks to get back.

(ARNIE *comes in with cardboard box full of Marxist books; dumps them by the door.*)

He was very *angry* about Vietnam. He tried to rugby-tackle a police horse. He forgot it had two pairs of legs.

ARNIE: I don't know why we bother.

(INGY *comes in, stands by door.*)

The little sods never buy them.

INGY: They do sometimes.

(HUGH *gestures 'goodnight' with coffee-cup and goes out.*)

WILL: Shall we turn in?

CLAIRE: OK. Night.

(*They go off into the bedroom.*)

ARNIE: Was it something I said?

(INGY *hovering by the door.*)

INGY: No. I don't think so.

ARNIE: Right then.

INGY: OK.

ARNIE: There was something else. Oh, I know, the list. What the fuck did I do with it?

INGY: It's in your back pocket.

ARNIE: Oh, yeah.

(ARNIE *finds the list.* INGY *impassive.*)

Haven't got a sandwich or anything, have you? I could eat me granny if she's kosher.

(INGY *points to the tray.*)

INGY: There's some biscuits.

(ARNIE *swoops on the packet.*)

ARNIE: Amazin' innit? The Yids knock hell out of the Arabs and it doubles the price of shortcake.

(*Munches.* INGY *hangs by the door.*)

Fucking Zionists. They'll kill us all before they've finished.

(INGY *runs her fingers through her hair, looks nervy.*)
Cheer up.
(ARNIE *goes to portable TV on table in front of sofa, switches on.*
Stares for a few seconds. Gun-fire, cheering and screaming from
telly. INGY *wanders over, drawn. Both watch a few moments.*)
Viva fucking Maria. For the third time this year. I wish it
was as easy as that . . .
(ARNIE *sits.*)

INGY: It's shit.
ARNIE: Yeah, but it's a laugh, innit?
INGY: All the revolutionaries are very beautiful look, very
bronzed. And everybody maintains their sense of humour
throughout. Like Hugh.
ARNIE: You know old Hugh, when he first took the papers round
Bolton House, he said – I don't think he'd ever been inside a
tower block before – he said, 'Why do they piss in the lifts,
Arnie?'
(ARNIE *chuckles. Both watch the television grimly. Then* INGY
reaches forward and pushes in the button. Sound dies.)

INGY: It's shit.
ARNIE: Cheer up.
(INGY *smiles wanly, drags her hand through her hair.*)
We'll have the bastards out by the spring.
INGY: Bastards. There are three and a half million now working
short time.
(*Pause.* ARNIE *looks at his toes. They're together on the sofa, but*
a fair distance apart.)
ARNIE: You've gotta keep calm about it. It's a political situation.
All these contradictions can be resolved.
(*Pause.*)
You're very tense.
(*Pause.*)
You know, this crisis goes down very deep. It gets to you,
inside.
(*Pause.* INGY *picking at her finger nail, trying to tear off a split*
corner. ARNIE *moves closer, hand along the back of the sofa.*)
Gormley reckons if the miners go on strike it will strengthen
the Tories. That's your working-class leadership.

(*Hand round* INGY's *shoulder.*)
They'll sort him out.

INGY: Don't touch me.

(*Pause.* ARNIE *fiddles with the packet.*)

ARNIE: D'you want a biscuit?

(INGY *shakes her head.*)

INGY: In Germany there are ex-SA brownshirts teaching in the universities! The NPD Nazis have guns.

ARNIE: Yeah well, there's this terrific upsurge of reaction at the moment.

INGY: There's no time to prepare!

(ARNIE *tries to hug her.*)

INGY: Don't touch me!

ARNIE: I was just trying to tell you it's all right.

INGY: It's not all right! Don't touch me, don't touch me, don't touch me!

ARNIE: I'm not. I'm not touching you.

(*Long pause.* INGY *screwed up into a ball.*)

INGY: I'm sorry.

(*Pause.* ARNIE *gets up.*)

ARNIE: Right then. I'll go through the list. It's changed since you last did the locals. 28, Harrington Gardens. Hasn't been seen for about three weeks. Isn't answering the door. Could be in retreat, but try him. Most of these are fairly close together. 112, Bagley's – that's an actor. He's just got a big telly part and he reckons he doesn't want to know us. So give him a hard time. That comrade in Bolton House, Flat 17. He lives next to a fronter with a fuckin' big Alsatian. They're not allowed to keep dogs but everybody's too scared to tell him. Just zap it through the letter box and use the lift double quick. He'll pay in due course. He comes to meetings, he's an old comrade from the Labour split days. But whatever you do don't ring the fuckin' bell. That's about all. The rest you'll recognize. Gaitskill House is a bit of a jog. If there's anything worrying you, take another comrade along with you. How many papers you got here? Forty. Should be enough.

(*Pause.*)

INGY: OK.

ARNIE: I'll be off then.

> (*Pause.* INGY *still on the sofa.* ARNIE *by the door. Waits a second, goes.* INGY *unwinds, blows out her cheeks. Unzips her jeans, rests her hand in there for a few seconds. Takes it out. Goes to her shoulder bag. Takes out two Mogadon. Sips some left-over chocolate. Takes the pills. Switches off the lights in turn. Just the light through the hall door. Goes out. Bedroom door opens. Light spills out.* CLAIRE *runs across the darkened room to get a sleeping pill from her handbag.*)

WILL: (*Off*) Mmmmm!

CLAIRE: Oh, God, I'd better take half. I've got to be up at six.

> (*Loud banging on the outside door, off.*)

Oh, no, who the hell's that?

WILL: One of Hugh's chickens come home to roost.

> (CLAIRE *leans against the door, listening. Voices off.*)

Maybe they've come for us at last.

> (*Voices off.* HUGH *comes on with* BUFFO, *almost supporting him. He's carrying a very old Gladstone bag.* HUGH *guides him to the sofa.*)

BUFFO: I wouldn't trouble you. I wouldn't trouble you . . .

CLAIRE: Oh, no Buffo . . .

> (HUGH *makes a keep calm gesture to* CLAIRE.)

CLAIRE: What's wrong?

BUFFO: Just my life, my life . . .

CLAIRE: Is it Tod?

BUFFO: Yes, yes . . .

> (WILL *in from the bedroom.*)

CLAIRE: He was coming *home* today.

BUFFO: Yes.

CLAIRE: What happened?

BUFFO: I don't know. It's all over. I can tell you that.

> (HUGH *has brought him a gin.* BUFFO *takes it, salutes the company.*)

Cheers.

> (*Gulps it down.*)

He *is* home.

> (*Embarrassed pause.*)

He came home at six. With an orderly.

CLAIRE: Is he all right?

BUFFO: Fit as a fiddle.

(*Pause. He takes the rest of the gin.*)

Thanks. I needed that.

(HUGH *takes the glass, goes to refill it.*)

He's a young orderly. Very kind. I thought he'd go. Eventually.

(*Pause.*)

BUFFO: I realized about half an hour ago . . . he wasn't going home. I could have stayed but . . .

(*Looks at* HUGH.)

I brought a few things. I thought I might borrow your sofa.

HUGH: Yes, of course.

CLAIRE: I'll give you a valium. Then you'll get a good night's sleep.

BUFFO: (*Almost losing control*) Tod was very proud of him. He's a shop steward. He led the strike. He nearly *died* while this bastard was trying to milk the hospital board for a few drachmas. While this *Greek* was saving up for his third stereo and a pair of fancy aluminium wheels for his *Datsun*. (CLAIRE *gives him a pill.* HUGH *hands him a glass with some gin in it.*)

WILL: That's Ingy's bag.

BUFFO: Will this knock me cold? Is it a Mickey Finn?

CLAIRE: No more gin after that.

HUGH: You'll have sweet dreams.

WILL: Where did you get the bag. Buff?

BUFFO: I don't know. Is it one of yours?

WILL: I think it's Ingy's bag. Remember?

HUGH: I don't know.

CLAIRE: I think it is.

BUFFO: Well you know me . . . I may have borrowed it for something. It's been around a few months. I thought it was Tod's.

CLAIRE: Yes, look. M. L. Lutz.

WILL: She went barmy when she lost it.

BUFFO: Look, I'll take my things out. I've only got a few

intimate *toiletries* and a towel. As we used to say in the army.

(BUFFO *takes out his toilet bag, a towel.*)

I have a feeling I'll be travelling light when I reach the pearly gates.

HUGH: I shouldn't worry too much. He nearly snuffed it. It's probably a reaction.

BUFFO: Maybe, maybe.

HUGH: You can kip in my bed. I'll doss down here.

BUFFO: I expect it'll all blow over.

HUGH: If you go to bed now, you'll miss Claire telling you it's the economic crisis that's to blame.

BUFFO: In that case . . .

(HUGH *moves to the door.* BUFFO *gets up, follows.*)

You're very kind. You're a good lot.

(HUGH *guides him out through the door.*)

HUGH: I'll tuck you up, Buff.

BUFFO: I think you're right Hugh. I think we *do* need a strong government . . .

(WILL *and* CLAIRE *look slightly askance at the last remark, but decide they really hadn't heard it.* CLAIRE *has picked up the bag and is examining it.*)

CLAIRE: Some papers in here. Tucked in a pocket. Buffo must have missed them.

WILL: Probably her speech notes for some long forgotten meeting of the West Brompton Young Socialists. She's so fucking diligent, that girl.

(CLAIRE *is reading the papers, carefully. Preoccupied.*)

CLAIRE: I don't like this.

WILL: Well, she's never going to win a speechwriting contest.

CLAIRE: No. It's a list. It's a list of names and addresses of people in the party.

WILL: Careless.

CLAIRE: It's not just a few. There are two or three thousand names here. Some names even I don't know.

WILL: It could have come from the centre, couldn't it?

CLAIRE: No, no. They'd never let anything like this out. It's absolutely forbidden to keep names.

WILL: Now, look . . .

CLAIRE: No, I mean it, Will . . . This isn't a joke.

WILL: Calm down. Let's think about it . . .

CLAIRE: No. I'm going to get her up . . .

WILL: Oh, come on, you saw the state she was in.

CLAIRE: She'll be in a worse state when I've finished.

WILL: There's an explanation. There always is.

CLAIRE: We'll find out.

WILL: You're going to make a bloody idiot of yourself again.

CLAIRE: Let go. *You're not controlling me!*

> (*She breaks free and rushes out.* HUGH *comes in. Giggles, hand over mouth.*)

HUGH: Ooops. This looks fun. Having another one?

> (WILL *gestures.*)

> Get it over with quick, eh? I want to go to sleep.

WILL: God help us all. And Tiny Tim.

HUGH: What's wrong?

WILL: I can't even begin . . .

> (CLAIRE *comes back in with* INGY, *in night things.*)

INGY: I thought it had gone for good.

> (*She opens the bag, looks inside.*)

> Couldn't it wait till morning? I had a sleeping pill.

> (CLAIRE *very calm, picks up the list.*)

CLAIRE: What's this?

INGY: I don't know.

> (*She turns to* HUGH, *shows him the bag.*)

> It was my father's. He died when I was two.

CLAIRE: It's a list.

INGY: Ja?

CLAIRE: People's names and addresses.

INGY: I don't remember.

CLAIRE: People in the party, fellow travellers.

INGY: Yeah, so?

CLAIRE: So we're forbidden to keep names and addresses. They can fall into the wrong hands.

INGY: I know, I forget. If you give it to me I'll burn them.

CLAIRE: No, not yet.

INGY: It was stupid. But look, they're safe. So, it's OK.

CLAIRE: They've been typed.

INGY: I don't remember typing them.

CLAIRE: Our names are on this list, and this address.

INGY: Of course.

CLAIRE: And about two thousand others.

INGY: I needed them for some work I was doing for the party. When was it, January, last year?

CLAIRE: What, Manchester, Leicester, Glasgow addresses?

INGY: (*Unconvincing*) I was asked to check up on the work the branches were doing. How many paper sales. What was the recruitment rate. How many YS meetings. That sort of thing.

CLAIRE: Oh, I see.

(WILL *and* HUGH *are keeping in the background. Not wanting to take a lead. But* WILL *has the* angst, HUGH *is at present treating it as a joke.*)

INGY: I had to have everybody's address.

CLAIRE: Yes, of course.

(*Pause. She sits at the round table, with the list.*)

Why is Hugh's name here?

INGY: I don't know. Why shouldn't it be?

CLAIRE: You made the list a year ago. He joined us last spring.

INGY: He was sympathetic.

CLAIRE: Yes, you knew that. But would the centre know? And what's more would they be so unprincipled as to put his name on a list?

HUGH: Keep me out of this. Please.

CLAIRE: You're in it, chum. You're involved. You're on the list. It's *your* business.

HUGH: I think you need a decent night's sleep.

CLAIRE: I can check, Ingy. I can phone Jimmy or Elaine at the centre. They'll tell me if you're telling the truth.

INGY: I don't mind.

CLAIRE: What's the number, Will?

(*She pulls the phone across the table.*)

INGY: 267 4932.

(*Pause.* CLAIRE *holds it for a few seconds, thinking. Begins to dial.*)

153

CLAIRE: Thanks.

(INGY *starts to cry, quietly.* CLAIRE *gently replaces the receiver. Very long pause.*)

WILL: Christ.

CLAIRE: Look, Ingy . . .

(INGY *shakes her head, in tears.* CLAIRE *much softer.*)

CLAIRE: It's much easier if you tell us the truth, pet.

INGY: I want to say this. The party is *correct*.

CLAIRE: No. Not all the time. We make mistakes.

INGY: Our analysis of the situation is better, more principled. We are the only party capable of giving leadership to the working class. We are the only party that sees beyond grass roots struggles. I want to say this. I want this to be understood.

HUGH: I don't understand anything.

CLAIRE: Why don't you want me to ring the office?

HUGH: There won't be anybody there now. Only a guard. This is just fascistic bullying.

CLAIRE: (*Calmly*) I'm not bullying. I want Ingy to explain the list.

HUGH: She's told you. Don't you trust anybody? Do you want a Scotch or something?

INGY: No. I had two Mogadon.

(CLAIRE *fiddles with the papers.* INGY *is shivering.* CLAIRE *gets one of the blankets from the sofa, puts it round her.*)

INGY: Thanks.

CLAIRE: Come and sit at the table.

(INGY *moves, groggily.*)

INGY: Maybe I'll have a bottle of beer. My throat's dry.

WILL: (*Quietly*) I don't believe this. I don't believe this is happening.

(HUGH *opens a can of lager. Puts it in front of her.*)

CLAIRE: OK?

(INGY *nods, takes a sip of beer. A lot of the time she stares at the table. Occasionally she looks at the others, as if looking for sympathy.* WILL *sits at the table too, but looking away most of the time, or down at the floor.* HUGH *sits apart from the other three, and upstage. Watching with an almost elated curiosity which is very incongruous.*)

INGY: When I was at Frankfurt University, the big movement there was the SDS – the Sozialistischer Deutsches Studentenbund. It had a lot of factions, it was always splitting.

(HUGH *laughs*.)

What's so funny?

(HUGH *shrugs, turns away*.)

There was a lot of protest, Vietnam you know, but all they did was put a lot of students on the governing body and that killed it. So there was a faction there that was for more direct action, you know (*Laughs*) – acting defensively against fascism.

CLAIRE: What did that involve?

INGY: Burning cars, throwing eggs, shooting off gas pistols. It was completely stupid.

CLAIRE: But you weren't in that faction?

INGY: I did get involved with illegal actions. Really it was through a boy I was with. He was later arrested. Ennslin and Baader made a fire in Schneider store, for which they were arrested. We were involved in a small way, in the conspiracy. But the police left us alone, I don't know why. Anyway I got frightened. Ulrike and Baader, they were crazies. They called themselves Communists, but they didn't go near the working class. Which is why the working class won't free them from Stammheim gaol. They made things bad for everybody on the left. If you bought Ulrike a hamburger in '65 you were arrested. So I tried to get a place to study here. I was pretty lucky to get one.

(*Pause.* HUGH *goes across the room and pours himself a drink*.)

When I was in England, I came to Wembley, to the pageant. I couldn't believe how strong this movement was. I remember this guy stood up in a spotlight, it was after about three hours of the play. He said, 'My name is Karl Marx.' And ten thousand people stood up and cheered. There was so much confidence. And so, you know, I joined the League and then the RSP. It's my life, you know, up to here. But then my course finished. I don't want to go back to Germany. So I'm staying here illegally. When I was at the other place, with the wallpaper, you know, there was a boy there. He worked at a builder's merchant. He was quite friendly. I tried to get him to come to meetings, you know, we talked politics. But I don't know, after a while I got suspicious. His politics were very weird. I tried not to have too much to do with him.

(INGY *has a long drink.*)

One day when I got back to my room, there were three guys there. I'd been working late at a delicatessen. There was one young guy, in jeans and a sweatshirt and two older guys, very straight, about forty. They were Special Branch. They had a file from the Frankfurt police. They had a lot of information. Some guy had informed. Baader had borrowed his Mercedes and smashed it up, so he gave the police a lot of names for spite – real liberal, you know.

(HUGH *laughs, very quietly.*)

They said give us information about the League, or we'll send you home and you'll go to gaol. It was around the time of Saltley. And Ulrike Meinhoff had been caught and some of the faction had died in strange fashions. I was pretty scared of reprisals. I argued all night. I said I wasn't scared of going back. But they could tell, you know, I *was* scared. So I agreed.

CLAIRE: Ingy.

INGY: Just to get rid of them. Because I thought I could just give them anything and stuff that would confuse them.

CLAIRE: This wouldn't confuse a child.

(*Fiddles with the list.* WILL *is shaking his head gently.*)

INGY: I tried to play a sort of game. Giving them descriptions of meetings that didn't happen. And I confused all the policies deliberately. I tell you I started to get confused myself. But it didn't work. I tell you, they've got some pretty sharp theorist up there somewhere. They're not as stupid as you might think. They're university guys. They knew I was fooling them. They got very heavy again. So then I was in very deep. They wanted names and names of sympathizers too, and names of anybody who gave money. So I said I was making this list, but I never got to hand it over.

CLAIRE: Is that the truth?

INGY: I thought, if they put pressure again, I'll tell someone.

CLAIRE: But they could have picked you up at a meeting. Anytime.

INGY: Yeah, I know. In the end I thought I'd rather be picked up than tell anybody in the party.

CLAIRE: Why do you think they didn't? It seems incredible.

INGY: I don't think so.

CLAIRE: Why not?

INGY: Because of the IRA bombs in London.

(*Pause. She puts her head forward on to her arms on the table, rests there.*)

We were irrelevant. We're not tourists.

(CLAIRE *stands up, goes across the room. Pours a drink.*)

WILL: What are we going to do?

CLAIRE: I don't know. I've never been in this situation before.

INGY: I couldn't get involved with any other movement. I don't think there's any other chance for the working class.

CLAIRE: I must think, think.

(INGY *is still slumped forward.* WILL *gets up.* HUGH *moves to sit at the table upstage of* INGY.)

HUGH: Don't worry.

(*Ruffles her hair. No response.*)

It wasn't your fault.

(*Looks at the others. Puts a hand on* INGY's *head again. No response.*)

Come on . . .

(*He lifts her head.*)

She's out of it.

CLAIRE: Put her into bed.

(WILL *lifts her up easily, takes her out.*)

HUGH: Well, spycatcher?

CLAIRE: She'll have to go to the centre tomorrow and be interrogated properly. I don't know what to believe.

HUGH: Interrogated? Oh, honestly . . .

CLAIRE: You really haven't caught on, have you?

HUGH: What's going to happen then?

CLAIRE: Nothing. They'll just expel her. We couldn't have

anybody that's had any connection with a terrorist group. It's impossible.

(CLAIRE *goes back to the telephone.* WILL *comes back in.*)

CLAIRE: I'm going to ring Jimmy. I can't handle this on my own.

HUGH: I'll just nip out and load my armalite, in case they try to spring her.

CLAIRE: This is serious!

(CLAIRE *picks up the phone, and dials.*)

(*To* WILL) You'd better keep an eye on her.

(WILL *nods dumbly, turns round and goes out again, almost automatically.* HUGH *is laughing.*)

This is serious, Hugh.

(*Phone ringing still.* CLAIRE *holding on, has turned her back to* HUGH. HUGH *has grabbed the rug and has pulled it round him. Lights fade, music crossfades.*)

CLAIRE: Hello. Listen, I'm sorry to bother you . . .

(*To black.*)

SCENE 5

1 March 1974. 12.30 a.m. In black, Billie Holliday, 'Some Other Spring'. Fade up quickly. TV sound. BUFFO *watching Sony.*

ROBIN DAY: So. Now. After that, let's go over to Bob McKenzie for his analysis.

MCKENZIE: Well Robin, early days, of course, but on the strength of the half-dozen or so results we have in so far – it's a very definite swing to Labour, of around 2.9%, not enough to give them an overall majority, but it means these forty or so Tory seats are going to be in danger, that's these seats here in light blue. And if the swing to Labour was more, say 3.1%, we could see these seats here change hands as well. But we need more results, Robin.

ROBIN: Thank you, Bob McKenzie. Now over to Cheltenham, where I think we have news of a re-count . . .

(HUGH *comes in. Bath towel. Wet hair. Adjusts sound.*)

HUGH: I thought you were having an early night.

BUFFO: Chap called when you were out. Forgot to tell you. Envelope on the table.

HUGH: (*Ruffled*) Oh.

(*Goes to table, slits open envelope.* BUFFO *not looking. Takes out tiny fold of paper. Picks up* Revolution Betrayed, *slips it underneath. Slight smile.*)

BUFFO: He said it was 'good stuff'.

HUGH: Oh . . . good. (*Goes over to* BUFFO.) Er . . . listen, Buff. I didn't think you'd be getting up again. I've got a young lady coming round. Do you mind if . . .

BUFFO: Of course, of course.

(*Looks embarrassed.*)

I only got up because, er . . .

(*Phone rings.* HUGH *picks it up.*)

HUGH: Hello. Hi . . .

(BUFFO *gets up. Goes to door. Changes his mind. Goes to drinks.*)

HUGH: Oh, shit . . . heigh ho.

(BUFFO *pours a quick gin.*)

OK, yeah.

(BUFFO *goes out.*)

Well maybe Saturday. Uh, huh. Good.

(HUGH *laughs.*)

No, not any more . . . it's true! Yes!

(*Laughs grimly.*)

I've decided. Honestly. I just haven't done anything about it yet. It isn't exactly going to be easy. They don't take no for an answer as a rule.

(CLAIRE *comes in.* HUGH *notices.*)

Er . . . yes. (*Nervous laugh.*) Yes. I'll ring you. Sure. Bye then.

(CLAIRE *puts down bag, smiles.* HUGH *replaces the receiver, smiles.*)

HUGH: He's nice isn't he? (*Slightly camp.*) I'd vote for him.

CLAIRE: I just came home for a rest before the result. I've gotta go back.

HUGH: Well?

CLAIRE: Oh well, you know, I'll probably get about seven

159

hundred votes. But every one will have been worked for, and every one's a potential member.

(*Sits down, not looking at telly.*)

Did you get those leaflets round?

HUGH: Just about.

CLAIRE: My agent gave me the push today.

HUGH: What! Why?

CLAIRE: Doesn't like me turning down work.

(*Shrugs, lies back.*)

Not that I don't make her enough money as it is. It's just I'm an embarrassment. The sods that actually employ me don't mind. Silly cow, she is. She wanted to push me as a political singer. 'In the seventies,' she said, 'Women and politics . . .'

(*Puts her thumb and forefinger together in imitation.*)

HUGH: What's wrong with that?

CLAIRE: Look, History decides if a song is political or not, not my fucking manager.

HUGH: Example.

CLAIRE: 'We shall overcome.' Whatever happened to 'Power to the People'? They haven't got it yet. Who's going to give Peace a Chance? I'd rather sing 'Lover Man'. (*Sings*)

'A huggin ana kissin'

Oh, what I've been missin'

Lover man oh where can you be . . .'

(*Phone rings. CLAIRE picks it up quickly. Pips. Then dialling tone again.*)

Damn.

HUGH: I'm sorry, anyway.

CLAIRE: Oh, I'll survive. But then I'm not one of a hundred and fifty Juvenile Character Northern Working Class actors.

HUGH: No.

CLAIRE: There's a blacklist, you know.

HUGH: Well, I'm glad he turned out to be a good Bolshevik.

CLAIRE: So did you! You were much harder work. You're my big success.

(*Pause. CLAIRE is obviously expecting the phone to ring.*)

He's been working *so hard* up there.

(*Pause.* HUGH *fiddles. Looks at TV.*)

HUGH: Well, this all seems pretty irrelevant. I thought for the first time in my life things were actually happening. Now here we are gawping at Bob McKenzie.

CLAIRE: Look, the working class have brought down a government. That little git in the Gannex is actually going to have to do something for them.

HUGH: If he gets a majority.

CLAIRE: Where's the Socialist Programme? In the Labour Party Manifesto? We're providing the political leadership. We're bringing these policies into the open.

HUGH: I sort of feel I have a few political disagreements with the party now . . .

CLAIRE: Well bring them up . . .

HUGH: What I mean is . . .

CLAIRE: We're building a mass Revolutionary Party. It doesn't just reflect one point of view. That's the point of struggle, but you have to struggle within. Christ, I came home for a rest.

(*Phone rings.* CLAIRE *picks it up.* HUGH *gazes at the silent screen thoughtfully.*)

CLAIRE: Yes, Will . . .

HUGH: (*Quietly*) RSP gain in Paddington East. . . ? Somehow . . . I think . . . not.

CLAIRE: I can't hear you . . . what?

(CLAIRE *grimaces.*)

Yes . . . what? Oh . . . shit.

(*Waits a second, listens. Then puts down phone.*)

I couldn't understand what he was saying.

HUGH: Bad line.

CLAIRE: No . . . Something about not getting any sleep.

(*Door bell.* HUGH *goes for it.*)

HUGH: Being sent to Birmingham branch sounds like punishment enough. Poor bastard.

(*Goes out.* CLAIRE *sits down, looks worried. Picks up phone, about to dial. Thinks. Puts phone down. Voices off.* HUGH *comes back in, with* INGY. *She's carrying a Sainsbury's carrier bag.* CLAIRE *very cool.*)

INGY: I took some of your books by mistake. They got mixed up with mine.

CLAIRE: That's all right. You shouldn't have bothered . . .

INGY: I hate it when people do it to me.

(INGY *is rummaging in her bag.* HUGH *is by the door.*)

INGY: You might need them. *Where is Britain Going?* That was yours.

HUGH: You didn't nick my collected Borges did you?

(INGY *hands* CLAIRE *the book. Searches again.*)

CLAIRE: Oh, great, thanks . . .

INGY: (*With a blank look at* HUGH) No, I don't think so.

HUGH: Probably Arnie's dad. (*Laughs at his own joke*
INGY *has handed* CLAIRE *another book.*)

CLAIRE: I don't think this is mine, *Farewell My Lovely.*

INGY: I've got two copies.

CLAIRE: OK, well . . .

INGY: I've got nowhere to put them all . . .

(HUGH *and* CLAIRE *exchange glances.* HUGH *goes out.* INGY
rummages again.)

INGY: I got you a present.

CLAIRE: Oh, you . . .

INGY: I picked it up in Portobello.

CLAIRE: How are you?

INGY: I'm all right.

CLAIRE: Yes?

INGY: I'm all right.

(INGY *still searching her bag.*)

INGY: I applied to rejoin the party.

(CLAIRE *impassive.*)

I think I stand a good chance, don't you?

CLAIRE: I don't know.

INGY: Here it is.

CLAIRE: What is it?

INGY: I don't know. It's an anything. It's a box.

CLAIRE: Thanks.

INGY: You can keep things in it.

CLAIRE: Thanks.

INGY: It was very cheap.

(INGY *goes back to her carrier bag.*)

CLAIRE: What are you living on?

INGY: I just got fifty pounds from Germany. I'm OK.

(INGY *is spreading some objects on the table.*)

I got some amazing stuff.

CLAIRE: What's that?

INGY: Baby dress. Isn't it fantastic? Look at the embroidery. Look at those stitches.

CLAIRE: Are you thinking of having a baby?

INGY: No.

(*Goes back to the stuff.*)

And look, some 45s. 'Wooden Heart'. Remember that? In bad Deutsche, very sentimental.

(*Pause. Looks at* CLAIRE.)

It's weird coming back here.

CLAIRE: Where are you living?

INGY: I have to move around.

CLAIRE: At the moment.

INGY: Hugh found me this place.

CLAIRE: Did he?

INGY: Yeah, some commercial artist. He's got a studio in Putney. Used to be a stable.

CLAIRE: Hugh seems to have space for everyone.

INGY: That bastard Arnie fucked off again.

CLAIRE: Really? Who told you that?

INGY: He wouldn't speak to me, you know.

(*Pause.*)

His old man joined the CP.

CLAIRE: That I didn't know.

INGY: Yeah, his old man's living with a woman in Brentford. She's a shop steward at Trico.

CLAIRE: Windscreen wipers.

INGY: Right.

(*Pause.*)

It'll be so good to be back. In the thick.

CLAIRE: What happens when they find you?

INGY: This is a very important period we're passing through.

CLAIRE: You'll be deported, yes?

163

INGY: I've got a lawyer.

CLAIRE: How can you afford a lawyer?

INGY: He's a friend of Hugh's.

CLAIRE: I didn't need to ask, did I?

INGY: Hugh reckoned he owed him a favour. Bernie something.

CLAIRE: Bernie wouldn't do anything for nothing.

(*Pause.* CLAIRE *preoccupied.*)

INGY: He says it's a bit difficult. I got married under a false
name. And Arnie's fucked off. What do I do if they have to
find him in a hurry?

CLAIRE: I don't think you should get involved with politics,
Ingy. Until you've sorted this out.

INGY: It's not illegal. The guy who sells the paper, he wouldn't
let me buy one. That's really small-minded. What does he
think I'm going to do with it?

(CLAIRE *can't think of anything to say.*)

Could I ask you a favour? Could I have a bath?

CLAIRE: Well, I think Hugh's just had one . . .

INGY: I don't mind if it's cold.

CLAIRE: I'll find you a towel.

(CLAIRE *goes out.* INGY *goes across to the table. Idly picks up*
Revolution Betrayed. HUGH's *cocaine slips out.* HUGH *comes
in, dressed.* INGY *is fiddling with the packet, puts it down.*
HUGH *frozen.* INGY *goes back to looking at book.* HUGH
moves quickly, picks up coke without INGY *noticing.*)

INGY: Do you think I could borrow this?

HUGH: Sure.

(*Pause.*)

Ingy.

INGY: Ja?

HUGH: Can I ask you a question?

INGY: Yeah.

HUGH: Would you like to sleep with me tonight?

INGY: (*After a pause*) No thank you.

HUGH: OK. Fine. Just thought I'd ask.

INGY: That's OK.

(CLAIRE *back in with towel.*)

CLAIRE: Here.

(INGY *takes it*.)

INGY: Thanks.

(CLAIRE *goes out. Pause*.)

HUGH: I mean if you don't ask you don't get.

(BUFFO *comes in. Doesn't see* INGY.)

BUFFO: Hugh, can I have a little word . . .

(*Sees* INGY.) Oh, pardon me. Anybody fancy a little drink?

INGY: No thanks. I don't like to much.

BUFFO: Extraordinary.

INGY: Puritan upbringing. My folks were in this weird sect. The Wandervogel. They walked about in the woods and did wrestling. Hitler Youth with mysticism. They stopped it after the war.

BUFFO: Is that why you teamed up with these Anarcho-Syndicalists?

INGY: What?

BUFFO: Isn't that what you are?

INGY: Anarchists!

BUFFO: Oh no, I didn't quite mean . . .

INGY: We're Trotskyists. Communists.

(INGY *goes out, angry*.)

HUGH: You thought . . .

BUFFO: I don't know.

HUGH: I don't believe you.

BUFFO: I'm not a political animal.

HUGH: You just thought we were a bit extreme . . .

BUFFO: I get very confused nowadays.

HUGH: But what did you *think* about us then?

BUFFO: I thought you were a good crowd. Still do. People are either OK or they're not. Mostly not. Listen, this is a bit embarrassing . . .

(CLAIRE *comes in*.)

HUGH: Go on.

BUFFO: Later, later . . .

(*Goes out*.)

CLAIRE: You mustn't let her in again. It puts us in an impossible position.

HUGH: OK, well, I'll get a spyhole fitted.

CLAIRE: OK. Fine. Can we have some money for the fund? This economic crisis isn't going to go away, you know.

HUGH: But I feel, I have . . . a lot of differences now with the party.

CLAIRE: They're not fundamental.

HUGH: I think they are.

CLAIRE: You've been terrific these last few weeks. We have to build a leadership.

HUGH: I only joined for the girls really . . .

(CLAIRE *laughs.* HUGH *looks uncomfortable. Pause. He goes over to the table, searches. Finds his cheque book.*)

Fifty pounds?

(CLAIRE *pulls a face.*)

CLAIRE: Make it out to . . .

HUGH: I know . . . (*Writing*) . . . fifty pounds *only*.

(*Phone rings.* CLAIRE *picks it up, quickly.*)

CLAIRE: Hel—

(*Waits for the pips.* BUFFO *appears in the door. Pyjamas, dressing gown.*)

BUFFO: Hugh . . .

(*The pips go on, the phone cuts.*)

HUGH: What is it, Buffo?

(BUFFO *looks distraught.* HUGH *goes across, gives* CLAIRE *the cheque as she replaces the receiver, goes to* BUFFO.)

CLAIRE: Must be using a bent coin.

BUFFO: I've pissed the bed.

HUGH: Oh, don't worry, I've got some more sheets.

BUFFO: I'm sorry.

HUGH: Sit down, have a night-cap.

(BUFFO *sits at the sofa. Bottles and glasses are now on the low table, with the Sony.* BUFFO *pours a Scotch, grimaces. Looks at the box.*)

BUFFO: What's going on?

CLAIRE: Oh, it's just a General Election.

BUFFO: Now? God, time flies.

(HUGH *makes a 'he's been hitting the bottle' gesture to* CLAIRE *behind* BUFFO's *back.*)

Look at that oik, he looks like a ventriloquist's dummy.

HUGH: It is a ventriloquist's dummy.

BUFFO: No, I'm wrong, it's Lenny the Lion.

CLAIRE: Doing an impersonation of Angus Maude.

HUGH: Except it's Julian Amery.

CLAIRE: They all look the same to me.

BUFFO: You've been a good pal to me, and I hope what I'm going to say won't upset you. But I don't think I can stay here any longer.

HUGH: (*Trying to sound disappointed*) Oh, why . . . ?

BUFFO: I feel a bit of a shite after all you've done.

HUGH: I haven't done anything.

BUFFO: I keep thinking of it all going on up there. I've had a couple of offers, from old friends. Quite touching really. Got a little cottage on a game estate in Leicestershire. I hope I haven't caused you a lot of *angst*. Didn't know how to break it to you.

HUGH: Well, cheers. To your new life.

CLAIRE: I haven't got a drink, but . . .

(*She makes the gesture.*)

BUFFO: You're very kind.

(*Turns back to the telly.*)

Now look at him. Look at that absolute shite. He was in my college. He's a *complete thickie*. He used to be a Communist. We used to edit a magazine called the *Arch-Realist*. Well, to tell you the truth it was more arch than realist. There are gonna be a lot of shites on there tonight.

CLAIRE: You can see where he keeps his liquid assets.

BUFFO: Up his rectum, I shouldn't wonder. Safer than the bank it's so tight.

(*The hall door is open.* WILL *comes into view. He stands in the doorway. Donkey jacket, fawn cords, dirty. Looks as if he hasn't slept or washed for three days. He's carrying a rectangular box, wrapped in brown paper.* CLAIRE *leaps up.* WILL *has put the package down.*)

CLAIRE: Will . . .

(*He backs out again and disappears down the hall.* CLAIRE *goes out again after him.*)

BUFFO: What's the life expectancy among your lot?

HUGH: About thirty to thirty-five.

> (*Pause.* WILL *comes back in again quickly. He's carrying a glass of milk and a bottle. He puts it on the table, looks restlessly round the room.* CLAIRE *has followed him back at a slower pace and stands by the door, looking worried now.*)

CLAIRE: What are you doing in London?

> (WILL *gestures to her not to bother him. He looks at the bookcase, shakes his head a little, ambiguous.* CLAIRE *has picked up the parcel from the side table by the door.*)

WILL: Leave it!

> (CLAIRE *shrugs, puts it back.*)
>
> (*Mumbles*) Discipline.

BUFFO: Not my kink old boy.

WILL: (*To* BUFFO) Er . . . can you go and do that somewhere else?

BUFFO: I'll be gone tomorrow.

WILL: Well start now. I have to talk to these people.

BUFFO: I don't know thee, old man.

CLAIRE: You look out of your skull.

WILL: Haven't slept.

CLAIRE: Well go to bed now.

WILL: You think there's time to *sleep*?

> (*Goes out again, quickly.*)

CLAIRE: Jesus . . .

HUGH: Sorry about that, Buff . . .

> (*But* BUFFO *is quite engrossed in the election which is chuntering quietly on.*)

BUFFO: S'all right. I've been hounded all my life for being a queer. John Vassal's got a lot to answer for. It wouldn't surprise me if they didn't have files on us all . . . What did I do? I slept with a chap who slept with a boy who slept with a mongoose who slept with the Prince of Wales.

CLAIRE: Please, Buffo . . .

BUFFO: I didn't do it for sex. That's the crazy thing. I did it for comfort. I did it for company.

HUGH: I understand that, Buff.

BUFFO: We thought they were going to liberate us. So we all

joined the party. And what were they? Queer-bashers to a man.

HUGH: Is he all right?

CLAIRE: He just needs some sleep.

HUGH: Like everybody else it seems.

(WILL *comes back in.*)

WILL: Sorry, am I interrupting an important theoretical discussion?

CLAIRE: Where did you ring from?

WILL: I can't tell you that.

CLAIRE: Did you ring just now?

WILL: I was over the road. I had to see if you had company. The coin went through. So I had to risk it.

(WILL *looks around the room again.*)

I need your address book.

(CLAIRE *still by the door.*)

CLAIRE: What for?

WILL: We've got to be armed.

HUGH: But Vasily Vasilievitch, we only have ploughshares . . .

(WILL *grasps the phone lead and jerks it out of the wall.*)

I see . . .

WILL: Just in case anybody's silly enough to use it.

CLAIRE: What's in here?

(*She points to the package.* WILL *goes across to it.*)

WILL: Sorry, you haven't been trained.

(*He rips open the package with his back to* CLAIRE. *A replica Walther PPK in a brightly coloured box. He stuffs the box away. Shows* CLAIRE *the gun.*)

CLAIRE: You're absolutely forbidden to have firearms. Weapons of any sort. You *know* why.

WILL: (*Smiles*) I know.

HUGH: (*Quietly, to* CLAIRE) It's all right.

WILL: (*Shouting suddenly*) Why can't you all just leave me alone!

HUGH: It's a replica.

WILL: They're emptying prisons on the Isle of Wight. Been clearing them for the last month. For us. They're going to lock us up.

(CLAIRE *and* HUGH *exchange glances, recognition.*)

WILL: It's a State of Emergency. They don't even need to pass a law.

CLAIRE: And what about the working class, Will?

WILL: It's all right. We had a meeting. We discussed them.

CLAIRE: Where was the meeting?

WILL: Somewhere . . . I dunno.

CLAIRE: *Who* had a meeting?

WILL: It doesn't matter. We had a meeting.

CLAIRE: Who's we?

WILL: What has happened you see . . . has been a series of defeats . . . Lenin said, better to suffer defeat *with* the masses than remain neutral . . . either a . . . bourgeois military dictatorship or a workers' *armed* . . . democracy, there's no third way. And . . .

(*He stops, gesturing, as if he's forgotten where he is.* BUFFO *is watching the telly, oblivious.* WILL *moves quite normally to the round table, sits down. Feels in his coat pocket, pulls out a sandwich, wrapped in cellophane, starts to eat it.* CLAIRE *picks up the gun, throws it in the wastepaper basket.*)

CLAIRE: You don't want to play with that any more.

(WILL *carries on eating.*)

WILL: Just leave me alone, I'll be all right.

CLAIRE: How long have you been in London?

WILL: Eh?

CLAIRE: You've been in Birmingham. You've been ringing from there.

(WILL *smiles mysteriously, shakes his head.*)

Where *have* you been?

HUGH: Somebody would have missed him in Birmingham, if he hadn't turned up.

WILL: I conned them.

CLAIRE: Where have you been staying?

WILL: I can't tell you.

CLAIRE: Who have you been staying with?

WILL: Oh . . . you know. Just this chick.

(*Pause. Eats.*)

She was useful.

CLAIRE: I can't handle this.

WILL: We're not going to get another chance, are we. We
fucked it up.
CLAIRE: I can't handle this at all.
WILL: It had to be now.
(HUGH *has come forward with a drink of Scotch for* WILL.
But WILL *springs up.*)
HUGH: Have a slug of this . . .
WILL: *Now!*
CLAIRE: (*Screaming*) *Where have you been?*
BUFFO: Steady on.
WILL: *Now!*
(BUFFO *looks over his shoulder, shakes his head in annoyance.
Turns the box up very loud. An election result being announced,
cheers and applause. Labour gain.* WILL *throws himself at the
bookcase, starts to tear all the books off the shelves.* INGY
stands in doorway.)
WILL: Now, now, now, now, now, now, now, now.
(HUGH *and* CLAIRE *don't interfere. He is surrounded by
books.
Quickly to black.*)

SCENE 6

In blackout/change light.
Voice of old woman, educated Russian, slight French accent.
PRINCESS WOLKONSKY: . . . And the house was invaded by a
whole troop of Bolsheviks, with rifles and machine guns.
And the head of them said that we were all to be taken at
once to the GPU, or more or less shot. And my father said,
'But why?' And then suddenly he had the idea of saying,
'But isn't it lunch-time? Perhaps you would like something
to eat?' and they all looked at each other and said 'But yes,
en effet, it's lunch-time.' And so we went down, and luckily
everything was ready. And they said, 'But you are charming
people. We don't understand why you are to be shot.' So
they left one chap and they went off to see if we really had
to be shot. And that chap, my father gave him a quantity of

wine – and he got complete drunk. And we didn't wait for the Bolsheviks to come back . . .

(*Fade up.* HUGH *is on a chair replacing the books. The Heath model is knocked over and is buried beneath papers and books.* BUFFO *is wandering around restlessly. Quite drunk.*)

. . . we went to the other end of the town where we had our racehorses.

BUFFO: Bad business. Saw a man go like that in the Admiralty.

HUGH: Why don't you go to bed?

BUFFO: It was the blinds. He hated Venetian blinds.

HUGH: Are you staying up for any reason?

BUFFO: I'd have him committed. Looks like he might turn dangerous.

HUGH: Go to bed, Buffo.

(BUFFO *goes to TV which is off. Flicks it on, burst of election sound.*)

BUFFO: Aaagh!

(*Switches it off again. Wanders back to* HUGH *who is inspecting the books carefully. Putting them back in some order.*)

Bloody boring rubbish. Depressing charade. Why do they let that boy play with that silly swing thing?

(*No response.*)

BUFFO: Who did you vote for?

HUGH: I didn't. I overslept.

BUFFO: Eh?

HUGH: Beddy byes.

(BUFFO *looks dejected.*)

BUFFO: I er . . . peed right through to the mattress.

HUGH: That's all right. Just turn it over. A new mattress, a new life.

BUFFO: Hadn't thought of that. You're a white man.

(INGY *comes out of the bedroom off. Closes door quietly.*)

INGY: OK. He's asleep now.

BUFFO: That was quite an arm lock you employed there.

(INGY *ignores him.*)

Well, I'll love you and leave you.

(*Turns at the door.*)

There's a simple road to happiness. Steer clear of politics and literature.

(*Slight pause.*)

And don't form any strong personal attachments.

(*Goes.* INGY *gives slight wry smile.*)

HUGH: You can stay the night if you want. It's a long way to walk.

INGY: Where?

HUGH: My room.

(*Pause.*)

It's all right, I'm staying up to watch the election.

INGY: OK. Thanks.

(CLAIRE *comes in. Very smart. Restrained, quite fashionable clothes. Quite a lot of make-up.*)

I'll er . . . get my things together.

HUGH: (*To* CLAIRE) You're not going out now?

CLAIRE: I have to be at the Town Hall. It's nearly two.

INGY: I thought maybe I'd come with you. For the results.

CLAIRE: I'd rather you didn't.

INGY: OK, yeah. I'd better wait 'til they decide my case.

(INGY *goes.*)

HUGH: He's very screwed up. He's really very poorly.

CLAIRE: It's just exhaustion. You don't mind looking after him tonight, do you?

HUGH: (*Wearily*) Great.

(*Pause.* CLAIRE *fiddles with piano.*)

CLAIRE: He's been with his wife and kids.

HUGH: How do you know?

CLAIRE: I can *smell* her.

HUGH: Why don't you practise any more?

CLAIRE: I do.

HUGH: The piano's a semitone out.

CLAIRE: She probably chucked him out. Don't blame her. He'll have to sort himself out. Here I go again. Think I'll stay single.

(*She moves across to* HUGH *quite close and looks at him intensely.*)

You've been a real support. Thanks. How did your campaigning go?

173

HUGH: I didn't go out. I had a hangover.

CLAIRE: (*Stunned*) What. . . ?

HUGH: I didn't even vote.

CLAIRE: Why not?

HUGH: I'm leaving the party. I think it's authoritarian and not a little unrealistic. Maybe I really did join for the girls.

CLAIRE: Oh, come on . . .

HUGH: I learnt a lot about politics, but it's too much like hard work. And there isn't going to be a revolution until I'm too old to care about it. So I'm getting out before I go round the bend too.

CLAIRE: That was just *liberal* anger. He doesn't want a revolution now. He just wants it to be over and done with so he can give up struggling.

HUGH: Why do you want life to be so hard? A million British soldiers got killed so our generation could have it easy.

CLAIRE: That's disgusting.

(*Moves away from him.*)

You can't just slip the party off like a used condom. What's next? Back to mysticism?

HUGH: I'll let you know.

CLAIRE: It just feels like a personal betrayal . . . God, that's so weak. (*Almost in tears.*)

HUGH: It isn't a betrayal.

(*Doorbell rings.*)

CLAIRE: We've got to talk about this, Hugh. You don't know what it's like to change, really change. I'm not worried about being middle class any more. It's the only thing he had over me. All my interests are with the working class. They're like my . . .

HUGH: Football team.

CLAIRE: If you like. But I can't go back on the old life now. That's my lift.

(*Collects her bag.*)

Marxism is a science. It explains the world, matter, everything.

(*Bell rings again.* HUGH *takes in the last remark, thinking.*)

I suppose I better move out.

HUGH: No. I think I will, for a while.

CLAIRE: (*At the door*) We must talk . . .

(CLAIRE *goes.* HUGH *blows out his cheeks in exhausted relief. Then goes to bookshelf and finds mirror, razor blade and straw. He takes out the small packet of cocaine. He opens it up. Hears someone outside and places Trotsky's* Where is Britain Going? *like a tent round the cocaine.* ARNIE *comes in.*)

HUGH: How did *you* get in?

ARNIE: (*Holding up key*) I keep forgetting to give it back.

HUGH: I suppose you've got the entire Central Committee outside.

ARNIE: I just came to touch you for some money.

HUGH: I've just . . . Will you go away if I write you a cheque?

ARNIE: We're not going to go away, Hugh.

(HUGH *finds cheque book. Starts to write.*)

What are you doing with yourself now?

HUGH: (*Through his teeth*) Editing an anthology of suicide notes.

(*Hands over cheque.*)

There you are.

ARNIE: You haven't signed it.

HUGH: (*Snatches it back*) I thought you'd disappeared.

ARNIE: (*Taking cheque*) No, mate, I've been sorting them out in Glasgow. Problem with you lot is you gossip too much.

HUGH: You mean your old man hasn't become a Stalinist and got shacked up?

ARNIE: This, I'm afraid, is true. He has.

(ARNIE'*s moving to the door when the upturned book catches his eye.*)

Oh, *Where is Britain Going?* . . .

(ARNIE *scoops up the book and knocks the cocaine on to the floor. He throws the book down again.*)

I wouldn't mind, only she isn't even Jewish. See ya!

(ARNIE *goes.* HUGH *mouths 'Fuck'. Leans against the table, defeated. Goes to TV, turns sound up. Goes off to the hall.* HUGH *returns with a toothbrush. On TV, sound of victory interview with Harold Wilson.*)

175

WILSON: (*TV*) The first thing to do is get the miners back to work! But before that we better get you all back to work! (*Loud, drunken cheers.*)

(HUGH *begins laboriously to pick up cocaine with a toothbrush. Fade in Burl Ives singing 'The Big Rock Candy Mountain'. 'The cops have wooden legs etc. . . .'*)